It's No Se<
THERE'S
Money
in SMALL
BUSINESS

Earn More. Work Less.
Enjoy What You Do Each Day.

Tyson E. Franklin

"A slew of new business books come onto the market near enough every month, each one assuring the secret ingredients to success and riches. Discerning which are useful and which are a waste of your time is a daunting task. Too many in this space are out of touch and only write to sell books.

"I've found Tyson's books wonderful, with down-to-earth honesty and a wealth of sound ideas, giving a new meaning to the idea of business planning, development and marketing.

"There are an abundance of opinions on business success and many great books about 'how', but a lot lack authenticity and proven application – I found Tyson's tried and tested ways handy and practical."

Dean S. Hawkins (author of *Fight Fire With Fire*)

"Whether you're just thinking about starting a business, already operating one, or you want and need to build your profits before selling your operation, you have to read *It's No Secret... There's Money in Small Business*. Tyson Franklin not only understands business and how to make one work, he also has an uncanny ability to show us how to enjoy business life even more and, simply put, how to make more money. You can't read this book without smiling, laughing, and increasing the value of your business."

David M. Frees (Trusts, Estates & Wealth Preservation Lawyer, Author of *The Language of Parenting*, Co-Host In Top Form TV & Podcast)

"Tyson covers a lot of ground in this book and provides very simple guidance that will give new business start ups what they need most – peace and faith. In starting a business, everyone gets overwhelmed and stuck at some point and this book will help them progress. But for every business that does start, there are so many that never take the first step. I feel this book will help a massive amount of non-starters get rolling with confidence. It gave me a lot of good reminders, and by the time I got a third of the way through the book, I felt this is a guide I need to give every friend who says, 'Hey, so I have this idea for a business…'. Well done Tyson, thanks for bringing this book to us!"

Kevin Miller (business owner and host of The Ziglar Show)

"I'm a big fan of Tyson Franklin's work. I applaud his down-to-earth and get-it-done attitude. If you are looking for a no-fluff, high action-oriented read, this book is for you."

Kathryn Kemp Guylay (Coach, Bestselling and Award-Winning Author, and Entrepreneur at Make Everything Fun)

"This book is not some wishy-washy 10-step program, or a bunch of theories. No, Tyson gives you real and raw advice from being in the trenches as a small business owner, giving you the real-life blueprint of the strategies and mindset of how you can be successful in all walks of life."

Mark Minard (CEO of Dreamshine, #1 Bestselling Author of *The Story of You*, Speaker, and Host of Elevating Beyond podcast)

"Too many business books spend too much time talking up why the advice they're offering is so important, instead of actually offering it with a plan of action. Tyson Franklin decisively delivers the latter in *It's No Secret... There's Money in Small Business*. His straight-shooting style cuts through the noise in your head and asks you to take action immediately with his practical advice. If you're not where you want to be in your business right now, allow Tyson's real-world experience to guide you out of your rut and on to the road of success."

Omar Zenhom (CEO and Co-Founder of The $100 MBA and WebinarNinja)

"Tyson Franklin is an inspiration to me and everyone whose lives he has touched. He's smart, funny, persistent, and passionately dedicated to sharing what he has learned in his business life with other small business owners. *It's No Secret... There's Money in Small Business* is a tour de force for anyone in small business (10M or less). Tyson provides a blueprint for success regardless of your specific business niche. This is the one book we all need to read and reread."

Rem Jackson (CEO Top Practices)

ACKNOWLEDGEMENTS

My wife Christine and my children have always encouraged my writing endeavours, and I truly thank them for this, even though my daughter Tia, who is currently 13 years old, thinks she's a better writer than me, and creatively she probably is. I can't wait to read her first book one day.

My older brother Tony Franklin is one of the most intelligent people I know, and even though we don't see each other too often, we speak a lot on the phone and some of the ideas in this book have come directly from our conversations.

I would also like to acknowledge two close friends that I've had a lot of coffee with over the past 12 months: Dean Hawkins and Nicky Jurd. Little do they know how much influence they have over my day-to-day thinking and how this has influenced the outcome of this book.

Deb Johnstone from Transformational Pathways Australia has also been a great help in keeping my head screwed on. We often have doubts about our abilities, and Deb has always managed to keep me focused on what I needed to do next.

My publisher Michael Hanrahan has made me feel like I can do anything when it comes to writing, and I can't thank him enough. His encouragement during the whole writing process has been very much appreciated, and he was also able to keep me on a strict timeline. Without his guidance and occasional nudging this book would still be in my head.

And finally I want to thank four people who are totally oblivious to how much they inspire me: Dr. Brent Seaver, Rem Jackson, Tom Foster and David M Frees, my American brothers from another mother. They are four people I'm lucky to call friends.

DEDICATION

I dedicate this book to Trish Franklin, my mother, who instilled in me a truly amazing work ethic. I was brought up believing that if you want something you must work for it, but more importantly she taught me about delayed gratification. Even though she may never have used this term, she did teach me you need to work first then enjoy the rewards. It doesn't work in reverse.

First Published in Australia in 2017 by
Proarch Franchising Pty Ltd
PO Box 39E
Earlville Qld 4870

National Library of Australia Cataloguing-in-Publication entry:

  Creator: Franklin, Tyson E., author.
  Title: It's no secret... there's money in small business.
  ISBN: 9781925648416 (paperback).
  Subjects: Small business.
          Small business – Management.
          Success in business.

Cover design by Peter Reardon
Internal design by Michael Hanrahan Publishing

Disclaimer

The material in this publication is of the nature of general comment only, and
does not represent professional advice. It is not intended to provide specific
guidance for particular circumstances and it should not be relied on as the basis
for any decision to take action or not take action on any matter which it covers.
Readers should obtain professional advice where appropriate, before making any
such decision. To the maximum extent permitted by law, the author and publisher
disclaim all responsibility and liability to any person, arising directly or indirectly
from any person taking or not taking action based on the information in this
publication.

CONTENTS

PART II: MARKETING

INTRODUCTION

You and I had a choice: to be an employee, or start our own business. And if you're reading this book I'm assuming you chose the latter, or you're at least considering it – and I believe that is the right decision. There's nothing more fulfilling than working for yourself and being your own boss. But, at the same time it can be a little scary, and you may even have some doubt, but don't be concerned… that's perfectly normal.

I always knew I wanted to work for myself, and I started my first business at 22 years of age. Like many business owners with no experience, I made a ton of mistakes, but I never let that deter me or scare me into thinking life would be easier if I worked for someone else. Instead, I used it to inspire me.

It's no secret…there's money in small business – in fact, there's *a lot* of money in small business, but having a high IQ or being a master of your trade or profession does not give you a right of passage to business success. This is a skill that must be acquired.

> "There has never been a better time, in the history
> of time, than right now to start a business."
>
> Gary Vaynerchuk

I'm sure there are business owners who will tell you that small business is tough, and they're correct: it *is* tough. But the one thing most small business owners forget is that every *big* business was once a small business, just like you. Nike, Coca-Cola, Ford, McDonald's, Apple and Microsoft all began as small businesses; in fact, some were so bad they probably should have thrown in the towel after the first year, but they didn't.

Coca-Cola was started in 1886 by Pharmacist Dr. John S. Pemberton, and in the first year of trade they averaged nine drink sales per day, adding up to a massive $50 for the year. In that same year they spent $73.96 on advertising, so it was definitely not a financial success in the first year. Most businesses do it tough in the first few years, and as you can see Coca-Cola was no different, but move ahead 131 years and Coca-Cola is selling more than 1.9 *billion* drinks per day and has a market capitalisation of $188 billion. Could you imagine if Dr. Pemberton decided to give up after one year, because it was too difficult?

Nike's early beginnings were no different. In 1964, University of Oregon track athlete Phil Knight teamed up with his coach Bill Bowerman, and together they sold a Japanese shoe called Onitsuka Tiger (now ASICS) from the boot of their car at athletic meets, and in their first year they made $8000, a far cry from what Nike as a company does today.

If you let history be your guide, many of today's billion-dollar companies had tough times in the early years and at some point looked like they were not going to make it, but they did. Even Apple did it tough in the late eighties and early nineties, but they rebounded and are today one of the most valuable brands in the world. Who doesn't own an iSomething?

"YOU CAN'T BE BIG WITHOUT FIRST BEING SMALL"

That's the way nature works and that's the way business works. Getting big all starts with changing the way you think. If you think like a big business, you'll start to behave like a big business, but this doesn't mean you must become a big business if you don't want to. But there are certain things big businesses do that every business should do if they want to be successful. And I'm not measuring success by how much money you make. Success means different things to different people – success for you could mean more time with your family, more holidays, or doing more for charities.

THE MOST COMMON SMALL BUSINESS MISTAKES

So where do small business owners most often go wrong? Firstly, they fail to delegate and try to do everything themselves. I'm not sure if they do this because they're control freaks; this may be the case, and I know I have been guilty of this myself. Or, maybe they're trying to save money by keeping the size of their team to a minimum. For most it's probably a combination of both.

Secondly, small business owners fail to invest money in their own education. I know when you're starting out in business or if you've had a few lean years you may not be flush with cash to attend conferences and tradeshows, especially if there's travel and accommodation involved, but if you're serious about being successful in small business you need to find a way to attend these events.

However, if you seriously have no money there is an alternative. You need to invest your time. Go online and start educating yourself. Start reading blogs, articles and listening to audio recordings, podcasts and watching videos. There is so much free information available online it's ridiculous, so there's no excuse for not doing this.

I listen to a lot of podcasts myself, and on 30 August 2016 I started the 365 Hour Mental and Physical Challenge. Basically I walk for one hour every day, and while walking I listen to a podcast, and then I shoot a short video sharing at least one takeaway point. I edit the videos and then post them on Facebook, YouTube and other online platforms. If I miss a day, it has to be made up, so the goal is to stay on track for the whole 365 days. *By the time you read this I will have finished my first 365 hours.* I say "first" 365 hours, as I may keep going.

The reason I tell you this is because I've learnt so much from podcasts, and I know you can do the same. Listening to someone talk about their mistakes and errors in business can make you feel so much better about your own stuff ups, and it makes you realise you're not alone. Not every podcast has to be about business either. I listen to a huge array of podcasts. Some are focused on personal development, and others are for pure entertainment and fun, but I still manage to learn something. Listening to podcasts even gave me the desire to start my own podcast series, which is called *It's No Secret with Dr. T.*

Here's the secret sauce though: when you invest in yourself things always change for the better, never for the worse. Now investing in yourself does not mean attending get-rich-quick seminars; it's about becoming a better version of your current self. Regardless of the type of business you own, it can always be improved upon, and this can only happen by opening your eyes and being prepared to learn. Become a student of business and life. You may need more knowledge about your products, your processes, or understanding your people. The goal is to keep your mind open for learning opportunities.

"Education doesn't just take place in stuffy classrooms and university buildings, it can happen everywhere, everyday to every person."

Richard Branson

To own and operate a successful small business you usually need to have some prior knowledge in the industry, and normally it takes years of training to become proficient, so it makes sense that if you want to have a successful business, you need to also be prepared to dedicate an adequate amount of time to acquire these new skills.

I've always had an interest in business, which is why I was reading *Making Money Made Simple*, by Noel Whittaker, in my spare time at university and not the usual textbooks other students were reading. Did this mean I cared more about making money than anything else? No, not at all, but I knew if I was going to work for myself one day and have a successful business, I had to learn more about business. Universities, TAFE colleges and apprenticeships are a great place to develop your skills and learn about your industry, but a terrible place to learn about running your own business. None of them prepare you for self-employment; they merely prepare you to be a competent employee. If you're serious about owning a successful business, you need to be prepared to understand the fundamentals of business.

I believe everyone deep down wants to be successful because the opposite of success is failure, and no one wants to be a failure, however only a small percentage of people are prepared to do what's necessary to achieve success. I once read that if you took all the wealth in the world and divided it equally among everyone, in five years' time the rich would be rich, the middle class would be middle class and the poor would be *complaining about all the rich bastards that ripped them off and stole all their money.*

The truth of the matter is, if you never learn how to make money, you'll never keep it. The rich would become rich again, not because they ripped off the poor, but because they know what it takes to become rich again and also how to do it. It's like riding a bike: once you know how, you can't unlearn this skill. Business and life skills are exactly the same.

If I had everything taken from me tomorrow, within 12 months I would rebuild because I know exactly what to do, because I've done it many times before, and I'm prepared to do whatever it takes to rebuild. Business success doesn't occur by osmosis, it's a learned skill and it's a skill you need to master.

I think it's important to point out that I didn't go to an expensive private school, instead I went to one of those public schools you read about in the news – for all the wrong reasons. However, my school did have some good attributes that many are unaware of. In one particular year my school held the record for the highest teenage pregnancy rate and also had one of the best football teams in the Brisbane district, so if you were male it was a great school. Seriously though, where you come from is not a predetermining factor of future success, it's where you see yourself going that's important. Having a private school education is no guarantee of success and – accordingly – going to a public school with a bad reputation is no excuse for failure.

If you're just starting out in business, or seriously considering it, I would highly recommend finding yourself a business coach, someone you can talk with on a regular basis, because working for yourself can be a very lonely place. Just make sure they have experience in owning their own business.

If you're a member of a state or national association, I think it's important to attend industry-specific conferences, expos and workshops, because you want to connect with other entrepreneurial people in the same industry if you can. I'm not sure how this happens, because there's no secret handshake that

I'm aware of, but entrepreneurial people seem to gravitate towards each other. You need to find them and hang out with them, because this is how you learn. You'll also notice the naysayers hang together as well, and you need to avoid them.

By the time you finish this book, I want you to have the confidence and belief that you too can have a great business in the future. If you've been in business for some time and you're already making good money, I hope after reading this book you'll be making even more, because if you're prepared to do the work then you deserve all the prosperity that comes with it. And you never know, the small business you own today may become a big business in the future. If Nike could do it, then so can you.

Let's get started!

Tyson E. Franklin

PART I
BUSINESS

1

BUT MY BUSINESS IS DIFFERENT...

If you're thinking to yourself, "but you don't get it, my business is different", you have to stop thinking this way, because it's not serving you well. Think about this; for every person who is doing it tough, there's someone else in the same profession or industry making a lot of money. Everyone has seen a restaurant close, while at the same time the restaurant next door is packed.

Why does this happen? Is it better food, do they have a better Head Chef, better staff, or maybe a better location? Yes, they could all be contributing factors, but I think there's a lot more to it than that. I think it's the attitude of the business owner.

> *"Whether you think you can or think you can't, either way you're right."*
>
> Henry Ford

In September 2016 I had a podiatrist approach me about employment. It was perfect timing because we were going to be one podiatrist down at the end of that month. After he was employed, he mentioned that he had handed his CV to another podiatry business in town and he showed me a text message he received in reply, which read:

Sorry, I received your CV and application for employment as a private podiatrist. Unfortunately due to the poor economic situation in Australia and in particular North Queensland, I am afraid you have come looking for work at the worst possible time. Maybe in a decade when/if the situation improves then maybe it will be a different situation. People are leaving the north in droves and it would be impossible to bring on a new podiatrist in the present situation. Best of luck in your search.

How on earth can you grow your business with such a bleak outlook and negative attitude towards your business and the town you live in? I find this text message funny, not because of the content, *because that's sad*, but because of the timing. I sold my podiatry business around this time – for a record sale amount for an individual podiatry business in Australia. What makes it more astonishing is the other business owner and I had similar qualifications, and our businesses were close to each other. So, you tell me, does your attitude play a role in your business success? I think it does.

> **"The best way to predict the future is to create it."**
>
> Peter Drucker

TAKING ACTION

If you want to have a successful business you need to take action, it's that simple. Too often business owners over-complicate this simple principle. Now you can *talk* about taking action and you can *think* about taking action, but until you actually take action nothing will happen.

YOU NEED TO SET BASIC BUSINESS GOALS

I think many people avoid setting goals because they over-think the whole goal-setting process. Writing a few goals down shouldn't be that difficult. For example, how much money do you want your business to turn over next financial year? If you're not sure how much, look at what you turned over this financial year and decide if you want to turn over *more* or if you want to turn over *less* than you did last year.

I think most business people do not want to turn over less than they did last financial year, so your first goal would therefore be to turn over more. So if you want to turn over more, how much more do you want that to be? You can choose a dollar value or a percentage, whatever works best for you. If you choose to use the percentage method, pick a value. Is it going to be a 1% increase or a 100% increase? It's really up to you, but once you select the percentage value for increased turnover, your goal is set – it is that simple.

Now comes the planning and breaking your goals down into smaller, manageable chunks. This is more difficult, but without first setting the bigger goal, you've got nowhere to start.

Using sport as an analogy is a great way to explain goals and why we need them. Could you imagine a soccer field with no goals at either end, and all you had were ten men or ten women running up and down the field for 90 minutes passing the ball to each other. *I say ten because there's now no need for a goalkeeper.* How boring would this game become for the spectators if there was no score. And yes sometimes there is no score in soccer, but because there's always the potential for scoring, this is what makes the game exciting. If soccer, basketball, football and many other sports all need goals to make the game worthwhile, then what makes you think goals are not important in your own life and business? Goals give you direction; goals give you something to aim at, and goals help motivate you to do more than you normally would without goals.

Goals need to be broken down into smaller chunks and planned into your busy life, but unfortunately it's right at this point where most people give up, but you shouldn't because you're so close. If you've found you've got to this stage in the past and stopped, get yourself a business coach, a mentor, or a business friend who can help walk you through this stage. It will be very worthwhile.

"A goal should scare you a little and excite you a lot."

Joe Vitale

Time needs to be allocated on a regular basis to review your goals, and research has proven that looking at your goals on a daily basis is by far the best strategy. I actually have my top five goals for the year as the header on my personal Facebook page because I know I look at it every day. If you don't use Facebook, come up with another strategy, but for me this works perfectly, plus it makes me accountable to all my family and friends and to anyone else who cares to see what my goals are. Are you brave enough to put your goals out there for everyone to see?

WHAT IS YOUR MORNING ROUTINE?

For my podcast *It's No Secret with Dr. T. (Episode 3)* I interviewed Wilson Lawrence, and he shared his thoughts around the concept of "The Morning Routine" and why it's so important. Your morning routine and how you start your day has an influence on your emotions and on your mood, so it's important to start your morning in the most positive way.

What do most people do when they wake up? They grab their phones, check their emails, and look at their social media pages. They're immediately consumed by technology. This is a bad way to start the day because it puts your mind in reactive mode, and you're now dragged into someone else's agenda. When you sleep your brain is recharged, it's revitalised, it's at its most creative, therefore first thing in the morning your brain is ready to do important work. Mornings should be used for reviewing your goals, planning your day, and prioritising your activities. Your morning routine should be about creation, not about consumption. Checking if someone "liked" the photo you posted last night is not important work.

If you don't do your most important work first, distractions will surely come along and prevent you from getting it done. We've all had days where we have so much time to complete one major task but by the end of the day we accomplished nothing, because we allowed one distraction after another get in our way. To stop this from happening, you need to look at your morning routine and make the required adjustments.

I would suggest listening to the whole Wilson Lawrence interview on my podcast It's No Secret with Dr. T., *and also his interview on the* Operation Self Reset *podcast with Jake Nawrocki.*

It's no secret…there's money in small business, but you need to take action, set goals and have a great morning routine.

After reading this chapter, what ideas are going through your head? Write them down *right now*.

_____

_____

_____

_____

_____

_____

_____

MOVING OUT OF YOUR COMFORT ZONE

Years ago, if someone had told me I'd be living in Cairns one day I would have laughed. Why would I leave the Gold Coast? It was my home and where I felt safe and comfortable...but here I am now in tropical North Queensland, and loving it.

My first business was on the Gold Coast, and it wasn't too successful. After four years I was making a living and that was about it. I had no business skills and my marketing consisted of placing an ad in the newspaper and phone directory, and putting up cheap signage. The thought of one day having a business that made hundreds of thousands of dollars profit each year never crossed my mind; back then I just wanted to pay the bills. Approximately three years into my career I suddenly developed psoriasis, and it became so bad I had to stop working altogether and eventually sell my business.

At the time it was devastating, but in hindsight it was the best thing that happened to me because it made me change the way I viewed business, which I'll explain in more detail later in the book. And I knew eventually my hands would improve and

I could start working again, which they did. After not working for almost two years, I began working at a hospital just to see how my hands would perform, and they were fine. I only worked at the hospital for six months, and it was one of the most brain-numbing experiences of my life. Talk about naysayers, negativity and small thinking. I don't know what every hospital is like, but I couldn't get out fast enough and start working for myself again.

I recalled some advice given to me by a university lecturer; he said if he was going to set up a business he would move to a regional area. Go to an area that's liveable and needs the skills that you offer, and to be more specific, he said he would move to Cairns. So I took his advice, packed up my family, and moved to Cairns in 1992.

My business in Cairns was a financial success from day one, even though my business knowledge had not changed, which goes to show that *any idiot can open a business and make good money if they open it in the right location – I was living proof.* So there's the contrast between staying in my comfort zone on the Gold Coast – where I made little money – and moving to Cairns, which was way outside my comfort zone, but I made good money right from the beginning.

Now don't get me wrong, I'm not saying that the Gold Coast was a terrible place to set up a business, but for me, at that particular point in my career, it was not a good place for me to be... *I was far too comfortable*, and I needed to move away so I could grow as a business person.

I know many business owners who make just enough money to keep them doing what they do, but not quite enough to really enjoy life, take their family on regular holidays, or do the other things they really want to do. As BCF would say, *"That's not living"*. Experience is telling them to make changes, but their lack of confidence won't allow them to. Instead they will do nothing, and over the next few decades, *yes decades*, they will make a few dollars

– just enough to get by – and eventually retire. Often these business owners become bitter and twisted towards life and other people who have done well financially, and will often say they must be breaking the rules, or they're dishonest.

So what are *your plans*? Are you planning to stay where you grew up and where you live now, possibly in *your* comfort zone, or are you prepared to move and live somewhere else? Are you going to open your business in an area that you're familiar with, or will you live on the edge and move outside your comfort zone? If you've been in business for a few years and it's not performing as well as you'd like, then maybe you should be asking yourself the same questions? *Because it's only when you move out of your comfort zone that amazing things happen.*

Moving out of your comfort zone though doesn't necessarily mean you have to relocate to another city as I did, it may simply mean you need to relocate your existing business to a better location.

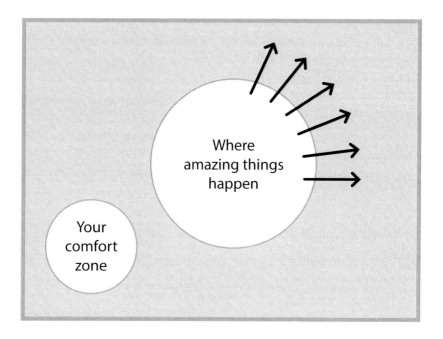

"Find your comfort zone, then leave it."

Robert Kiyosaki

CHOOSING THE RIGHT LOCATION

As a general rule, *the better the location, the higher the rent*, therefore it's unlikely your first business will be on a main road, so the next best thing is to find a road that is very familiar to everyone. If you're new to the area, simply ask people to name three connecting roads that are popular. If you're told the same connecting road multiple times then that should be the first area you investigate, however your budget is still going to determine your exact location.

Short-term thinking

Never think that your first location is going to be your last location and that you cannot move. Your business can be relocated every few years if extra space is required, which is why I suggest taking a short-term lease initially and also looking for a premises that requires very little fit out, because when you leave you cannot take the fit out with you.

The lease term of your premises will also be affected by any financing arrangements you have in place. If you take out a five-year loan with a finance company they will want the term of the lease to be at least five years, to match your repayments. However, if you have no finance you can do whatever you want.

These have been some of my moves over the years:

- My first business in Cairns was approximately 60 m^2 and I spent nothing on the fit out because it was already in place. *Perfect!*

- The last location (prior to selling my business), which was my fifth move over a 21-year period, was on the busiest road in Cairns, was 360 m², and I spent a lot on the fit out, however my wife and I own the building so the fit out is ours to keep, so once again, *perfect!* We now collect the rent; even more perfect.

- I established a business in Mackay. I took out a two-year lease and the location was approximately 50 m². The fit out was minimal because it was small, and by keeping our overheads to a minimum we made a profit from the first month, which was…you guessed it…*perfect!*

It's not uncommon to see businesses go bankrupt because they had visions of grandeur and their first location was far too large for their initial needs, which meant they had to over-borrow. *That's not perfect, that's stupid!*

> "Do one thing every day that scares you."
>
> Eleanor Roosevelt

SO WHAT MAKES A GOOD LOCATION?

Be easy to find

There is nothing more annoying than driving up and down a street looking for a business, especially if you're running late. Make sure your business is located near a distinguishable landmark or another business you can leverage from. "We're located next to the business with the large red car on the roof," is far easier than saying, "We're located at 3939 Elm Street and there's no number on the building". *Make sure you have a number on the front of your premises and make sure it's big.*

Have easy parking

The second most annoying thing after not being able to find a business is finding it and then not being able to find a car park within walking distance. A person may drive around in circles looking for a car park the first time, but they won't continue to do this if there are other options available to them – meaning a similar business with better parking. I get annoyed really easily by poor parking; how about you?

Have good signage

Regardless of your location, there needs to be an area where you can place some good signage, and if it can be illuminated at night that's even better. My first business on the Gold Coast had very poor signage opportunities, which probably contributed to its poor performance. In addition to this, my sign was positioned partly in a garden bed, which meant every three months I had to trim a few hedges, otherwise the sign could not be seen.

Have a good tenant mix

The tenant mix can be a location winner or a location killer. If you're looking at a premises in a small complex with mixed tenancies, consider who your neighbours are going to be. Having complementary businesses in the same complex can be a positive, however being located between a run-down tattoo parlour and a drug rehab centre may not be. You cannot guarantee who your neighbours will be in the future, but the current tenant mix is a good indication.

Stay at eye level

Your location should also take into account the age and agility of your clientele. Will your business be located on the ground floor or will it be on the first floor? Being on the ground floor makes for easier access and is much easier to find and see from the street. If you're considering the first floor of a building, is there an elevator, or only steps?

I remember a friend who had a business on the ground level. He had developed a considerable number of elderly clients, which was never his intention, and without thinking it through fully, he relocated his business to the first floor of the same building, meaning people had to walk up 25 steps to reach his front entrance. His goal was to reduce the number of older clients being able to reach him, which he achieved, however his overall client numbers also dropped significantly. He failed to consider the following when relocating upstairs:

- He lost his eye-catching street-level visibility, meaning people walking past didn't know he was there.

- He lost his signage positioning because it went to the new tenants who moved into his old position.

But the biggest killer, which he never considered, was a smart person noticed the relocation upstairs, so they opened a similar business across the road, at street level, directly opposite his old location, and they did very well. This new business was in a far better position and they picked up all the walking-by foot traffic, and in addition to this they immediately attracted all of his elderly clients that could not walk up 25 steps. It took more than two years for him to recover, and eventually he moved his business back to street level.

When it comes to choosing the right location you may not get it right the first time, but after reading this chapter hopefully you have some clarity and direction on where to look, and if you've been in business for some time and you think your current location may be part of the problem, don't wait until your lease is almost up before you start looking for a new location because it's never too early to start looking.

> "Your best teacher is your last mistake."
>
> Ralph Nader

It's no secret...there's money in small business, but first you need to venture outside of your comfort zone.

After reading this chapter, what ideas are going through your head? Write them down *right now*.

_____

_____

_____

_____

_____

_____

_____

_____

3

ADVISORS, INSURANCE, MONEY AND EQUIPMENT

ADVISORS

To have a successful small business you're going to need some expert advisors along the way, especially when it comes to financial and legal matters, therefore you need a good lawyer and a good accountant – I can't stress this point enough. Your lawyer will assist you with contracts in relation to financing, partnerships, equipment leases and renting premises, whereas your accountant will be required to ensure your business is structured correctly. For example, will you be a sole trader or a company? Do you require a family trust? These are very important decisions, which is why you need a lawyer and accountant immediately to help you with this.

I would also highly recommend getting a bookkeeper. You may find your accountant has a bookkeeper onsite; if not, ask for a recommendation. A bookkeeper will help you set up your financial records properly and will keep them in order. They will prepare your monthly profit & loss statements, prepare income activity statements, business activity statements, and also calculate your superannuation guarantee amounts. Even if you have no staff, you still must pay superannuation for yourself if you operate as a company. Your bookkeeper may also do your fortnightly wages, therefore calculating the amount of tax to deduct and accumulated holidays for full-time staff members. An important point to note: your bookkeeper charges far less than your accountant, so not only do they save you time, they also save you money. If you walk into your accountant's office with a shoebox full of receipts at the end of each financial year you will pay for your laziness, whereas if you have a bookkeeper you will provide your accountant with an electronic file containing all your financial information.

If you enjoy bookkeeping you can of course do it yourself. There are a lot of cloud-based accounting programs available, which require little bookkeeping knowledge, minimal training and are relatively inexpensive to purchase. As of 2017, Xero, MYOB, Quickbooks, Freshbooks and Zoho seem to be the most popular cloud-based programs. Obviously you'll save money by doing your own bookkeeping in house, and if you have team members available this can be a good option, but if you are a solo act, think about how you make money: is it by seeing clients or by crunching numbers?

You'll also get what you pay for, so never select an advisor or cloud-based program on price. Think about it; in your profession or trade are there any cheap competitors in your area? What's your opinion of them? Are they any good?

It's always a good idea to ask friends and family who they use for legal and financial advice and then ask why they use these particular advisors, and you want intelligent answers. When you're choosing an advisor, think of it like a job interview. You're actually interviewing them to make sure they are the right person for your particular needs. They are filling a position where you have an opening. If they come across as a "complete tool", even if they come highly recommended, I think you should look elsewhere.

If you have good advisors that's good news, however if you're not happy with them, change! I've had four accountants in my lifetime and I've had my current accountant for 13-plus years. My accountant is also now my brother's accountant, my brother-in-law's accountant and my son's accountant. What's important is that you find advisors you're comfortable with and you trust; your advisors are going to be a big part of your business life and they will know everything about you and your business, so trust is paramount.

INSURANCE

I know it's a pain in the butt and often people think it's a waste of money, but you need to get your insurances in order. Some insurance cannot be avoided, such as professional indemnity insurance, however it is tax deductible. If you have an employee, even for a few hours per week, you must have a Work Cover policy (this may vary from state to state, or be called something else outside of Australia). You need to do this immediately because if an injury occurs at work, or under some circumstances travelling to or from work, you may be held liable.

Work Cover only protects employees, it does not insure the business owner. Therefore, depending on your circumstances and commitments, you should consider income protection and business expense insurance as well. I used to think income protection insurance was a waste of money, especially when I was younger, but when I had my hand issues with psoriasis and could not work for two years I was glad I did have income protection and business expense insurance in place.

If you've borrowed money to finance your business, you may be asked by the financier to take out life insurance to cover the debt if anything happens to you, unless you have personal security or you've got a rich uncle prepared to be your guarantor.

With all agreements, especially insurance, always read the terms and conditions. Make sure you write down on a separate piece of paper anything an Insurance Agent says to you during your meetings that does not appear in the contract. Date it and have them sign it before they leave. If they will not sign it, you need to find another Insurance Agent who is going to be straight with you and not make stuff up just to get the sale.

When you add it all up, insurance is not cheap and many new business owners fail to take all their insurance premiums into account when they are preparing their budgets and cash flow forecasts. These additional costs can stifle your entrepreneurial spirit if you're not prepared for them.

> "Think of insurance this way; you're betting them
> something is going to go wrong and they're betting
> you it won't, but believe me your future self will
> thank you for making the right decision."
>
> Dr. T.

CASH IS KING

Many businesses struggle in their first few years because they've gone into the venture full of enthusiasm and then quickly run out of money. If you're considering opening a business right now, you should have enough cash in your bank account to cover all your business expenses for a minimum of three months; that's my thinking. Anything less than that and you're kidding yourself. Lack of funds is very stressful, and stress affects your judgment and decision-making capabilities. You want to build your business with a clear head, not a cloudy head concerned with paying next month's rent. Good cash flow allows you to pay all your accounts on time and also gives you the ability to purchase in bulk and make significant savings, especially on items you use on a regular basis. You will also save money on freight if you're ordering fewer times throughout the year.

Don't rush into opening a business if you don't have the cash flow. You are better to wait another 12 to 18 months and do it properly, because you also need to allow money for marketing. Marketing is a key component to your business success, and when you open your business you want to market it effectively. If you've been in business for yourself for a few years and it's not meeting your expectations, what's your monthly marketing budget and what's your attitude towards marketing? Do you look at marketing as an investment or an expense? This will be discussed in far more detail in Part II of this book.

INCOME-PRODUCING VS NON-INCOME-PRODUCING EQUIPMENT

When it comes to purchasing equipment for your business, there are two types of equipment purchases you can make. One is income-producing equipment and the other is non-income-producing equipment. For example, let's say you need to purchase eight chairs and you're deciding between a $150 chair and a $400 chair, which means you will spend $1200 or $3200. This is when you need to stop and think. Will the $150 chairs be sufficient for your current needs? If yes, can you use the $2000 saving elsewhere in your business?

I know from experience that you are better off investing $2000 towards income-producing equipment, because it will generate income from day one and will continue to do so for the life of the equipment, whereas a $400 chair will not.

Set equipment goals

Before making any equipment purchases, you must ask the following question: *"How long will it take before I get my full investment back?"* It's important to know the answer to this question before you purchase any equipment, for two reasons:

1   it will help you set your prices for the service

2   it will help you set realistic goals for when this will be achieved.

Purchasing equipment without setting realistic goals is ludicrous. I've seen business owners buy new equipment but never stop to consider how they were going to make money from it. This is a great way to go broke fast.

If you think about it, income-producing equipment can and should be used to set your business apart from your competition, and the type of equipment you purchase says a lot about you and your business.

What type of business do you want to have one day and how do you want to be perceived?

It's no secret...there's money in small business, however you must have great advisors and manage your finances.

After reading this chapter, what ideas are going through your head?
Write them down *right now*.

_____

_____

_____

_____

_____

_____

_____

_____

WHAT TYPE OF SMALL BUSINESS DO YOU WANT?

Opening your own business is a great decision, but have you given any thought to the *type* of business you want to have? This may sound like a strange question, and when I say "type of business" I'm not talking about deciding between starting a coffee shop and a bakery, even though that may be something you are currently considering. What I mean is, have you considered what you will offer in your particular business?

This simple thought process does three things:

1   It will help set your business apart from your competitors.

2   It will help you set your prices.

3   It will have a direct influence on the type of clientele you attract.

I'll use a coffee shop as an example to drive home this idea about the type of business you want. There's pretty much a coffee shop in every shopping centre and on every city street corner. Some are highly successful and others are not so successful. Have you thought about what sets them apart? It's true location can play a huge part in a coffee shop's success, but if they make rubbish coffee they will not last long, regardless of position. Successful independent coffee shops often roast their own coffee beans *their way*, or they source their coffee beans from a particular coffee roaster; they won't just use the cheapest or most convenient coffee bean supplier, which is important when they're competing against successful chain and franchised coffee shops. They may also source and offer a selection of high-end coffees from around the world.

By being selective in their coffee bean suppliers and coffee roasting techniques, it makes their coffee quite distinct from their competitors. This uniqueness allows them to set their prices slightly higher and therefore this will have an influence over the clientele they attract. If you're looking for a cheap cup of coffee and you don't care how it tastes this is probably not the coffee shop for you, but if you're a true lover of coffee and you care about how it tastes and you want variety from around the world, then this is your coffee shop.

If you're opening a restaurant, a bookkeeping business, or maybe a retail outlet, the same principles apply again and again. The type of business you want will either set you apart from your competitors or make you blend in with everyone else. It will determine what you charge and therefore the type of clientele you'll have to work with each and every day.

In the end, these three factors will determine how much enjoyment you get from your work each day, because you get to choose what your business will and won't do. A coffee shop may only serve premade cakes and tarts, or it could decide to have an onsite kitchen and serve meals. Once again it comes down to the type of business you want to have: will it set itself apart from your competitors? Can you charge more by offering additional services and will this attract the type of clientele you really want? Is your business aiming at quantity or quality?

"Quality is never an accident; it is always the
result of high intention, sincere effort, intelligent
direction, and skillful execution; it represents
the wise choice of many alternatives."

William A. Foster

GETTING YOUR RATIO RIGHT

To have a financially successful business you need to focus your
efforts into the areas of your business you enjoy most and the areas
that have the highest profit margin, and areas with a high dollar
value per hour – it's that simple. Don't get me wrong, every business owner can make good money by fulfilling the basic requirements of their profession or trade, but if you're not fulfilled with
your daily routine and you want a pay rise, you need to target your
daily efforts into the areas of your business with the best returns
and most enjoyment.

This doesn't mean you'll never do anything again in your
business that you don't like doing; it's more about getting the ratio
right between what you like to do and what you do not like to do.
If you're working all week doing work you despise, it's going to be
a long and uninspiring week, but if you can limit your exposure
to what you don't like it will make your week far more enjoyable.

For example, in my own profession there were things I did
not like doing, but before I knew this principle about *getting the
ratio right* I did them anyway because I knew no better. Eventually I got to the point where I wanted to leave my profession and
do something else, but a strange thing happened. When I limited
my exposure to the things I did not like to do and focused on
doing the things I did enjoy, work became more fun, I made more
money, I had more time off, and when I did have to do the things
I did not like to do, they didn't seem so bad after all, and doing

them on an occasional basis was actually enjoyable. It's funny how our minds work.

I would love to take full credit for coming up with this realisation about work ratios, however I first came across the idea after I attended a weekend seminar on how to have a more profitable business. After I attended this weekend seminar my thinking changed and so did my business. Within three months of attending this weekend seminar, my business turnover doubled and I never looked back. This is why I can't stress enough the importance of constantly educating yourself and why it's important to look outside of your own profession. This is why I also run my own events and weekend seminars, because I know how much they can help other business people. *For more information about my events please visit www.tysonfranklin.com.*

You may find it hard to believe that one weekend seminar made such a difference to my life, but that's all it takes. Unfortunately, you do not know which weekend seminar it is going to be! There's a saying, *"When the student is ready...the teacher will come"*, and this applies to everyone. I have spent a small fortune on self-education and development over the past twenty-five–plus years, and I will continue to do so because I understand the value. Hopefully you will see the value also.

If you're about to open your own business, now is the perfect time to start asking yourself, what type of business do you want? There is no right or wrong answer – you just need to decide, become focused, and then commit to it 100%. If you've been in business for some time and you're feeling a little trapped in what you've created, don't despair – just start making the required changes now and over time you'll see the benefits. Just like exercise, you won't see much change in the first few weeks, but after a few months the changes slowly start to become evident. Just be patient. (If you have any questions on this please send me an email: tf@tysonfranklin.com.)

"Success occurs when opportunity meets preparation."

Zig Ziglar

ARE YOU GOING TO BE AN ORIGINAL OR AN IMITATION?

Initially it can be difficult to know the type of business you want, so if you can't answer this right now, don't stress about it. Sometimes you have to just go with the flow and see what eventuates – just don't wait 10 years like I did before I came to the conclusion that I needed to change the way I was doing business. Unfortunately many business owners never get around to answering this question, which is why so many businesses are identical and constantly fight over the same clientele.

Is your plan to open another boring business, an imitation of what you've previously seen, or is your business going to be more *original*? Ask yourself the following questions about your proposed business:

- How many businesses in your area provide the same service?
- Are they all doing it the same way?
- Are they all using the same processes?
- What will distinguish your business from your competitors?
- What skills have you got that they don't?
- What equipment are you going to purchase?

If you cannot tell your business apart from your competitors, what chance do your clients have? Also, why would someone refer a friend or family member to you instead of to the business they've been using for the past few years if you're not offering something better?

If you want to have a successful business, you have to decide what type of business you want and you need to make an effort to stand out from the crowd.

"If you always do what you always did,
you will always get what you always got."

Albert Einstein

CHOOSING A BUSINESS NAME

Your business name is an important part of the identity of your business, and it can help to set you apart and demonstrate the type of business you are. Everyone wants a cool business name, but it's important to note that your business name is the first image that you put *"out there"* about your business, so it must be a reflection of the type of business you want to have one day.

Remember, your business name has the ability to attract or repel people, so you do need to give it some serious thought, but don't try to be too clever.

"Hanging a sign on a cow that says
'I am a horse' does not make it a horse."

Unknown

When it comes to creating a business name you should make sure it is easy to remember and easy to read. A simple name is a good name. It should also be unique if possible, and definitely not too generic. Avoid using the words that everyone else in your industry is using. For example, in the health industry using the word "clinic" or "centre" is common, but they are both nothing words and can make the business name sound very similar to others that use the same words.

Always check if someone else is using a similar business name to the one you are considering. A simple online search will show this, and you'll be surprised how many businesses have similar names. More and more people go online to look for services and search for information, so if they type in your business name, or something similar, will they get your business or will they get a competitor's business that sounds like yours? This can be frustrating if you've been busting your butt on advertising and marketing and your competitor is sitting on their butt and enjoying your efforts.

Can your business name grow with you? Does your business name contain your street address or city you operate in, and will this be a problem if you decide to expand in the future?

The jury is still out on business names deliberately spelt incorrectly. It may look clever but if you're having to constantly spell it out for someone so they can find you online because of odd, incorrect spelling, is it really a clever name, especially if it could be spelt correctly and have the exact same meaning? For example, I've spoken to business owners who have used Phyx instead of Fix and 4U instead of For You, and on both occasions they've had to clarify their business name and more importantly their website address. So, just be careful.

Once you have created your business name, you need to protect it because your business name does have value. Just having it registered in your state gives you no protection nationally, so the best option is to register it as a trademark. You can register a trademark over the internet yourself quite easily – which I have done on numerous occasions – or you can seek legal help, which may be the better option if you're concerned with doing it right, but this will cost you more.

It's no secret…there's money in small business, however you need to know the type of business you want and the type of clientele you want to attract.

After reading this chapter, what ideas are going through your head? Write them down *right now*.

_____

_____

_____

_____

_____

_____

_____

_____

DISCOUNTS, PRICE WARS AND ACCOUNTS

DISCOUNTING

Should you offer discounts? Discounting is a personal decision, and it really comes back to the type of business you want. If your business name contains the word "discount", and discounting is part of your marketing strategy, then you can skip this topic, but if you're being asked for discounts on a regular basis and that's not part of your strategy, then you may need to adjust your marketing because you're obviously attracting the wrong type of clientele. However, some people are simply discount chasers. Marc Mawhinney from the Natural Born Coaches podcast refers to them as "cheaple" (cheap-people).

There are certain groups of people who will often request a discount, because they've been educated to do so:

- pensioners

- seniors

- healthcare card holders

- people with a disability
- the unemployed.

But there's another group that everyone overlooks: "the tight arse". This group can afford your products and services but simply don't want to pay full price, and they will try to beat you down at every opportunity, or they'll ask if they get a discount if they buy two, and so on. What they fail to understand is how much discounts actually cost you.

The effect on your bottom line (know your numbers)

Many business owners don't see how discounting impacts their bottom line, which is why it's important to know your numbers. As a generalised example, if a product or service was $60 and if you had a profit margin of 30%, your gross profit would be $18 from that transaction. If you gave a client a small 10% discount of $6, so they only paid $54, this would be a 33% reduction to your gross profit, $18 *original profit* minus $6 *discount*, leaving you a profit of $12. If you gave them a 15% discount of $9, this would be a 50% reduction in your gross profit; $18 minus $9, leaving a profit of $9. The client only sees the small 10% or 15% discount; what they don't see is your bottom line and that you actually lose a massive 33% to 50% by discounting. (And, in all honesty, they don't care.)

A 50% loss in gross profits is lunacy and equates to you having to do twice the amount of work to make the same profits as another business that does not discount, which is why I think discounting to simply attract new clients is a crazy marketing technique.

Of course retail is a little different. If you're trying to move older stock to make way for new stock, such as footwear and clothing, then it makes perfect sense to have a discount in place, such as an "end of season sale".

PRICE WARS

If you have a new business open in your area and they are discounting their prices to attract new clients, don't try to compete by lowering your prices. Let them have their loss of profits and you concentrate on attracting clients who don't look for discounts and who would prefer a better service. Getting into a price war to attract new clients is one of the dumbest marketing strategies I've seen, and long term has to be detrimental to the morale of your team because they would constantly be working with people who have that discount mentality and who just want the cheapest price. *Getting into a price war with an idiot results in two idiots.*

If you have a business in your area that wants to start a price war, you should relish them because they will be filling their business with the *"cream of the crap"*, leaving you with all the high-quality clients.

SHOULD YOU PROVIDE ACCOUNTS?

I have the same account policy as the local supermarket: no accounts. If you can, you should adopt the same approach. Having a "no account policy" in my previous businesses meant my team did not have to waste time chasing outstanding accounts.

Of course some businesses must allow accounts, so if you're in that boat make sure you have strict guidelines and qualifying criteria in place. If your account policy is ever breached, don't accept excuses and don't give further credit if they're already behind in their payments. When I see an invoice that says 30, 60 and 90 days, this tells me you have 90 days to pay the account before it becomes overdue. Try changing your terms to 7, 14 and 21 days and see how much faster you get paid. If you're good at what you do, people will respect your new account payment terms and will join the party. If you want to protect your future, you need to value your services, charge accordingly, and get paid on time.

If you feel you need to discount, get involved in price wars and offer accounts to attract new clients and to keep your existing clients coming back, you have a business that is very sick and is in need of a big shot of penicillin.

> "Customers buy on price when they can't find
> extraordinary quality, convenience, service or value."
>
> Warren Greshes

It's no secret…there's money in small business, but you've got to avoid discounting.

After reading this chapter, what ideas are going through your head? Write them down *right now*.

_____

_____

_____

_____

_____

_____

_____

ATTRACTING THE RIGHT CLIENTS

THE BLOWFLY PRINCIPLE AND BAD CLIENTS

I don't care what type of business you have or how good your customer service is, you're going to eventually have a few difficult clients, the ones that make you want to stay in bed on a Monday morning and not go to work. And worst of all, they will think their behaviour is perfectly normal and acceptable, not realising they are complete tools. *I've had a few that come to mind immediately.*

So learning how to deal with difficult clients is really important, but it's not as important as learning how to identify them as early as possible. You need to learn that most difficult clients – actually let's call them what they are, "bad clients" – exhibit the same traits. See if any of the following sound familiar to you:

- they complain about your prices
- they are rude and stubborn (pig headed)
- they are always requesting discounts

- they ask for an account

- if you give them an account it will be paid late

- if you have an appointment system they turn up late without an explanation; however, they complain if you're running five minutes late

- they cancel their appointment at the last minute without a valid reason, and if you enquire they tell you it's none of your business

- they often "no show" for their appointments, once again with no valid reason

- they never apologise

- after cancelling, they complain if they cannot make another appointment for the following day, even after you've explained how busy you are

- making an appointment for them is always difficult because it doesn't fit in with their busy work, gym, or social schedule

- they complain and raise their voice at the most inopportune time, especially when there are other people around – they love an audience.

You know the clients I'm talking about. We've all had them and we will continue to have them, however your goal is to limit your exposure to them. You need to identify them early and get rid of them as soon as possible. If you can, you should redirect them to your competition, because if your competition is busy seeing all the Bad Clients, the ones you reject, just like John West, this frees up your time to see more Good Clients.

My brother is a Dentist and we refer to Bad Clients as Blow-flies, and together we have come up with a term called *The Blowfly Principle*. This may sound a little crude, but it fits perfectly for these types of clients. Let's say you're standing in your front yard talking to your neighbour and you notice dog poop on your foot-path. Nothing unusual there. Suddenly a blowfly passes in front of you and lands on the dog poop. Of course you keep talking and think nothing of it, but then all of a sudden something else flies past your face! What do you think it was?

Was it a bird? No!

Was it a plane? No!

Was it another blowfly? Yes, because blowflies attract more blowflies!

Bad Clients are similar to blowflies, because Bad Clients will attract more Bad Clients, because people associate socially with people who are similar to them. They'll talk about the weather, which movies they've seen and which services they like and dis-like. Bad Clients, if you keep them, will tell all their friends that you are the best business in the world because:

- they can arrive late and you never complain about it, which is perfect if the midday movie runs over the scheduled time

- they can cancel on the day without any penalty, which is important if the girls at the local club decide to meet for coffee and cake at the last minute

- if they decide not to attend at all because something better came up there is no penalty, which is perfect for those days when they just couldn't be bothered picking up the telephone and letting someone know they're not coming

- if they complain about their fees you will give them an immediate 10% discount, which is great because booze and cigarettes are getting expensive.

Do you really need to have these types of clients in your busi-ness, or would you prefer they visited your opposition? I politely removed many clients from my past businesses and I make no apologies for this, because it's my business and therefore everyone must play by my rules. You will find that Bad Clients, or blowflies, are a very small percentage of your total clientele and the majority of people will be a pleasure to work with, however it comes back to the type of business you want to have and how strict you are with discounts and accounts.

Remember…blowflies love a good discount and accounts.

"It is better to starve than get a bad client."

Massimo Vignelli

SO WHO IS YOUR TARGET MARKET?

If I asked you to picture your perfect client, who would that be? Do you have an image in your head, or is it a little fuzzy? Think about the following questions:

- What would they look like?
- What age group would they be in?
- Is there a specific gender?
- Would they play sport? If yes, what type of sports?
- Are they members of a gym or association?
- What's their income?
- Are they blue collar or white collar?
- What do they do socially?
- Are they members of any specific community groups?
- Where do they live?

The more questions you ask the more answers you get, and the more answers you get the better image you'll create of the perfect client. This mythical creature, the perfect client, does exist and they're waiting for you to find them.

Your perfect client is what's referred to as your *target market*.

Multiple target markets

If your image is still a little fuzzy it may be because you have more than one perfect client. You may have multiple perfect clients, you just didn't realise it. So, if there's a possibility that you may have two or three perfect clients then this also means you may have two or three target markets. Imagine a business, bursting at the seams with perfect clients, day after day – *how awesome would that be?* Not only would it be awesome, it would be a fun place to work and your pockets would be overflowing with cash.

I've heard business owners say their target market is broad, which basically means they have no idea about their target market. Well, actually that's not true – they do have a target market, *The Breathing*. Targeting The Breathing may sound like a smart move because you're covering all your bases, but it's very general and an ineffective way to try to market your business. Not having a defined target market is like playing darts without a dart board. You go through the motions and expend the same amount of energy, but in the end there is no result – it's a pointless activity.

Having a specific target market or multiple markets doesn't mean you will never see clients that do not fit your preferred target market, it just means you're focusing your marketing dollars and personal energy towards specific areas within your business that have been proven to generate great profit margins and a higher dollar per hour yield. When I first understood this concept of target marketing – or multiple target marketing – my business turnover dramatically increased and I enjoyed my work more each day.

This is not rocket science. When you know your target market and you focus your efforts and high-end services towards that target market, your hourly rate goes up and you make more money.

What services can you offer, or target, that produce great profits and have a high dollar yield per hour? This is what you need to consider if you really want to boost the profitability of your business.

"Everyone is not your customer."

Seth Godin

CLIENT TYPES A, B, C AND D

Understanding your target market or markets is important because if you don't know who you want to attract you'll waste money marketing to the wrong groups of people, but it's also important to understand that not everyone in your target market is going to be an ideal client. Just because a client fits into your target market doesn't mean they are going to be a client you want to keep. Within every target market there are also going to be distinct client types. For simplicity, I've divided them into A, B, C and D type clients. The longer you're in business, the easier it becomes to identify them.

Let's have a look.

A clients are your awesome clients. These clients make you want to get out of bed in the morning and be at work early. They always arrive on time, never complain about your prices, pay immediately, and they actually say *"thank you"* after the work is done, even after they have paid you. Their only drawback is their eagerness to refer other clients to you, which sounds great, but unless you educate them, they may send the wrong type of client.

B clients are good clients, but not quite as awesome as A clients. They do everything A clients do, just not at the same high level, yet they are still a pleasure to work with.

C clients are a pain in the butt. They arrive late without explanation, never apologise, they try to reschedule with little notice, they rarely follow your instructions and advice, and they complain about your prices always going up, even when they have not changed in two years.

D clients are rude, ignorant and are slightly more irritating than your C clients. C and D clients are basically Bad Clients, they are blowflies and should be redirected away from your business as soon as possible before they start referring more clients like themselves.

You should always try to work with your clients and at least attempt to upgrade them to the next level if you can. You should try to teach your C clients what they need to do to become a B client, so they can continue to be a client at your business, but if they are unwilling to make the required changes... refer them elsewhere. If you want to make good money and have a successful business you need to remove C and D type clients from your business.

Why you want more A and B clients and fewer C and D clients

Let's have a look at the many reasons why you need more A and B clients in your business:

■ You will get far more good referrals from A and B clients who gladly pay your fees, whereas C and D clients who think you overcharge will only refer blowflies.

■ A and B clients believe in what you do and they don't second-guess your motives. C and D clients will question everything.

- A and B clients show respect, whereas C and D clients don't.

- A and B clients expect good quality and are willing to pay for it. C and D clients want to be offered cheaper alternatives.

- When you put your prices up you do not need to explain yourself to A and B clients because they see value in the service you provide, whereas C and D clients will say, *"What, you're putting your prices up again?"*, even though it may have been two years since the previous fee increase.

- A and B clients make work fun because you get to utilise the full range of skills you have learnt. C and D clients will ask, *"Do I have to pay extra for that service?"*

- A and B clients will use your services again and again, whereas C and D clients only contact you when there is a problem or if there is a "special offer" on the table.

- A and B clients understand that additional services don't come free, whereas C and D clients will lie and say you told them it was included in the initial costs and there would be no additional charge.

- You build lifelong relationships with A and B clients, their family and friends, which will give your business longevity, whereas you never get to know anything about C and D clients other than their problems and complaints.

- A and B clients offer you constructive advice on how you could offer more services and make more money, whereas C and D clients will ask for discounts and offer you advice on how you could get more C and D clients by dropping your *ridiculous prices*.

- A and B clients allow you to make more money by working fewer hours, whereas C and D clients want you to make less money but work more hours.

- A and B clients love hearing about conferences you've attended, whereas C and D clients are not interested in your continued education.

Do you really need any further convincing? If you can fill your day with A and B clients there won't be room for C and D clients. And even if a few C and D clients manage to slip through your guard they will not stay very long because they will not like the positive vibe of you or your business – C and D clients love misery, and misery loves company, and that's not happening in your happy business.

"You can't make everyone happy, you're not a pizza."

Power of Positivity

It's no secret…there's money in small business, however you must surround yourself with the types of clients you want to work with.

After reading this chapter, what ideas are going through your head? Write them down *right now*.

_____

_____

_____

_____

_____

_____

_____

_____

THE VITAL FEW AND
TRIVIAL MANY

I first read about *the vital few and trivial many* in a magazine many years ago on a flight from Cairns to Sydney. I was on my way to attend a conference, and after reading the article I put the magazine down and gave it no further thought. However, on the first evening of the conference, after a full day of lectures and workshops, I watched the "Gods" (*Guest Speakers*) enter the post-conference venue – otherwise known as the bar – and I couldn't believe how quickly they were surrounded by other delegates eager to get a few minutes of their time, and how free drinks were thrust into their hands without them even asking. Then it hit me: I'd just witnessed the *vital few and trivial many* first hand. I couldn't wait to get back on that plane and read the article a second time, and when I did, it made sense.

In 1906 Italian Economist Vilfredo Pareto created a mathematical formula that described the unequal wealth in his country. He observed that 80% of the wealth was owned by 20% of the population. At the time this was called the *Pareto Principle.* Then, in the 1930s, Dr. Joseph Juran observed that 20% of all inputs, or activities, was always responsible for 80% of all outputs, or results. He called this principle the *"Vital Few and the Trivial Many"*. Both principles have since been used widely in business, management, engineering and science, and from these came the more commonly used term today: the 80:20 rule.

The 80:20 rule basically means:

- 80% of your headaches will come from 20% of your clients – *most likely your C and D clients*

- 80% of your business errors will come from 20% of your team – *which is why you need to constantly re-train*

- 80% of your client referrals will come from 20% of your referral sources – *you need to nurture these relationships*

- 80% of your income comes from 20% of the services you offer – *most likely your services with a high profit margin and high dollar yield per hour*

- 80% of your marketing will produce 20% of your results; however, 20% of your marketing will produce 80% of your results. (A process called *testing and measuring* will be discussed in a later chapter to help you figure out what is working and what isn't.)

This rule is by no means an exact science but it can be quite an accurate guide. But does it apply to your profession? *I'll let you be the judge of that, but I think it applies to most.*

Who are the vital few in your industry? They are the 20% who:

- earn significantly more money than the rest – healthy six-figure incomes

- have businesses that look very professional

- have businesses with modern and up-to-date equipment

- contribute to your industry and make things happen

- are involved in projects that will make a difference

- are regularly invited to speak at state, national and international conferences

- everyone knows their name

- everyone wants to be on their LinkedIn list

- everyone wants to be friends with them on Facebook and "likes" their business Facebook page

- everyone has them in their circles on Google+

- they're followed on Twitter because people want to know their opinion and thoughts

- people follow and read their blog posts

- their websites are alive, vibrant and constantly evolving

- they're givers, not takers

- they are always remembered after people have met them

- they will be sadly missed when they retire, leaving a significant gap to fill.

Who are the trivial many? They are the 80% that:

- earn the least amount of money *and they constantly complain about it*

- have businesses that look unprofessional

- have businesses with outdated equipment

- contribute nothing

- are never invited to speak at conferences, not even local events

- no one knows their name, and when introduced they are easily forgotten

- Facebook, Google+, Twitter, and blogs are ignored because no one cares about their posts or opinions

- their websites, if they have one, are under construction or out of date

- they are takers, not givers

- will not be missed when they retire; in fact no one will notice they have left because they will leave no gap.

Which group do you want to belong to? Not everyone can be a "God" who is invited to speak at national and international conferences, however you can still be one of the vital few who earns significantly more money than the average business owner. To do this you need to constantly remind yourself to stay focused on the 20% of your business activities that really matter and not get bogged down in the 80% that don't.

Building a successful business doesn't occur by accident, it begins by understanding and living by some simple proven principles, such as the 80:20 rule.

GETTING YOUR TEAM INVOLVED

As the business owner you may understand the importance of the 80:20 rule and how it can transform your business and make it more productive by focusing your time and energy on daily activities, the 20% that matter and avoiding the 80% that don't, however you need to get your team involved as well.

Team members often get *activity* and *productivity* mixed up, and often they spend too much time doing things that are not important, such as typing reports, checking the mail and emptying bins, which are all activities that do need to be done, however picking up the telephone and calling a client is far more important and it needs to be prioritised this way.

For this reason you need to offer guidance and leadership, and you should discuss the 80:20 rule over and over again at meetings. Discuss what activities belong in the 20% and what should be moved into the 80%. Make sure you get input from all team members and listen to what they have to say, then as a group formalise these two lists and make it a priority to constantly review them. Your 20% list should be far shorter than the 80% list; if not, you need to go back and look at your priorities.

Go to your diary right now and schedule this 80:20 meeting in. Don't ask your team when would it be convenient to have this meeting; instead tell them when it's on. This activity is far too important not to do, and when you do you'll immediately see results. Plus, it creates accountability. If you notice someone in your team doing unimportant 80% activities when they should be doing important 20% activities, you can go back to the 80:20 list *you all developed as a team* and use it for internal coaching purposes.

In Chapter 1, I discussed the importance of the morning routine when you wake up, but I think it's just as important for you and your team to have a morning routine when you're at your place of business. Every team member, including yourself, needs to do the most important tasks first. If you can combine the morning routine with the 80:20 rule, you're going to develop a very efficient team. A stressful day normally equates to a busy day, and most business people become busy when they focus on quantity instead of quality. It's not about being busy, it's about being efficient.

"Efficiency is intelligent laziness."

David Dunham

It's no secret…there's money in small business, however you need to know where the money comes from by understanding the 80:20 rule.

> **After reading this chapter, what ideas are going through your head? Write them down *right now*.**
>
> _____
>
> _____
>
> _____
>
> _____
>
> _____
>
> _____
>
> _____

SELECTING THE RIGHT TEAM MEMBERS

FRONT OFFICE PERSON

Your front office position is crucial and should not be taken lightly. A Receptionist is more than just someone who answers the telephone and organises your schedule. They actually represent you and your business, and they are the first person your clients see when they enter your business. Even with the best advice, guidance and screening processes, you can never guarantee the person you employ is going to be right for you and your business. I have employed Receptionists using ads in the local newspaper, by word of mouth, and I have used the services of a professional employment agency. Regardless of the method, some Receptionists have been great and others have been not so great.

When you're hiring someone as your Receptionist you should immediately pay attention to appearance. They must dress appropriately for the industry you're in. Their hair should be tidy and their nails should be clean, because what you see at this first interview is as good as it's going to get – it will never improve from that first meeting.

Your Receptionist needs a warm and welcoming personality, and they should be very comfortable using the telephone. Up-to-date computer skills are a must, and good grammar is also very important, especially if you want them proofreading marketing materials you've developed, and at times you may need them to write something on your behalf.

At interviews I like to ask two simple questions: "Tell me what you know about [add your profession here]," and, "What did you think of our website?" The first question seems obvious, but you'll be surprised how often people will apply for a job and know nothing about the industry, which surprises me because who seriously applies for a position in a field they know nothing about, or without having done at least a little homework about the industry?

The second question, in my opinion, is more important than the first, because it shows initiative and a little forward thinking.

It's rare for a successful business not to have a website, so it makes sense to at least look at your possible future employer's website to get an idea of what it is they do. If I was applying for a position I cared about, I would do my homework and also look at their website in some detail; however, if it was just a job to me and I didn't care, I would do neither.

I do a lot of business mentoring, and when someone makes their first enquiry with me via email, I go straight to their website to see who I will be talking with. I become concerned if there is no website.

Once you have identified the right person for the position, make them aware that there is a probationary period and make sure you do regular reviews of their work. If it's not working out, replace them; don't keep hoping things will improve because they rarely do. I have hung onto Receptionists and other team members' way longer than I should have and it always ends poorly.

An employee's success or failure though can often come down to your training methods, or lack of training methods, so make sure you have good training manuals and make sure all procedures and protocols are documented and are easy to follow.

SPECIALISED EMPLOYEES

When it comes to employing people with specialised skills the same rules apply as with appearance and dress sense, however in addition to all of the above they must also be able to communicate with their clients.

Their previous work history will give you a good indication about who they are. If someone had a sales job previously, they may come with good sales skills, and if someone worked behind a bar they may have great communication skills, but if their previous employment avoided all human contact, you may find they have no personality and have poor communication skills. Without these they will find it difficult working with their clients, and long term they will fail to impress.

Their lack of communication skills may also make it difficult for them to fit in with the rest of your team, which is extremely important if the team needs to work together. Always keep team coherence top of mind when introducing new members to an existing team.

It's no secret…there's money in small business, however you need a strong, effective team that works together.

After reading this chapter, what ideas are going through your head? Write them down *right now*.

_____

_____

_____

_____

_____

_____

_____

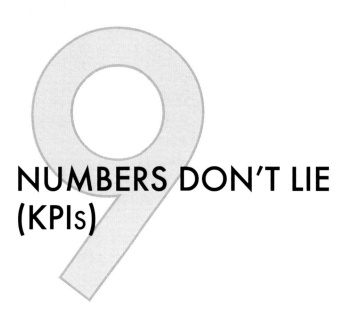

NUMBERS DON'T LIE
(KPIs)

When I owned my business on the Gold Coast I had no understanding about the relationship between business profits and business performance. I came to realise that even a poorly run business can still make a profit, however it could make far more profits if the business owners had key performance indicators (KPIs) in place to measure performance, because numbers don't lie, only people lie. KPIs can be used to identify people and processes within a business that are underperforming. They can also be used to measure progress towards business goals by looking at critical numbers on a daily, weekly and monthly basis.

If you've never considered using KPIs it may take a while for you to really appreciate their value, however once you see how they can transform an average business into an awesome business, you'll be convinced. An interesting thing happens when you start measuring KPIs; both your personal and business performance improve. This improvement occurs as a direct result of knowing your numbers, because *you can only improve upon something once you have a number to improve upon.*

For example, if you averaged 93 sales per month last July, your KPI for this July could be broken down as follows: 93 sales divided by 31 days for the month of July equates to 3 sales per day.

So on day 7 you would expect 21 sales or more, and by day 14 it should be 42 sales or more, and so on for the month. By knowing these key performance indicators you can immediately tell at any given point in the month, on a daily basis, if you are on track to surpass the previous year or if you are falling behind. Now this particular KPI includes the whole team, but it can be broken down to each team member, department, workgroup, regional office, state and so on.

WHAT SHOULD YOU MEASURE?

I don't think you can have too many KPIs, because the more information you have about your business the more educated your business decisions – but you also need to be practical.

Because every industry has different requirements, you need to work out what is the most important information you need each day, week and month. The above example was based purely on sales numbers, but for your business it could be:

- email enquiries
- online product orders
- number of people walking through the front door
- number of incoming phone calls
- number of outgoing phone calls
- new bookings
- building approvals
- sales contracts.

Every business will have certain KPIs that trump others. In the health industry new patients is always a massive KPI, as is re-booking numbers. What are your trump KPIs in your industry, the ones that are super important over and above everything else?

If you're planning on having a business with multiple locations, you really need to understand the power of KPIs and you need to have an extensive list of KPIs in place. I was once asked if you can have too many KPIs and the answer is no. You should have KPIs on every aspect of your business, then once you know the numbers you can then determine if they are important to continue with or not.

KPIs CAN HELP IDENTIFY UNDERPERFORMERS

Once you start looking at your weekly KPIs, underperforming team members will be found out very quickly, which is why it's important for all team members to be aware that you have KPIs in place. Don't keep it a secret; it needs to be common knowledge and the results need to be published somewhere, such as the lunchroom noticeboard, so they can be viewed by everyone. It's amazing how performance improves when everyone is held accountable.

KPIs CAN HELP IDENTIFY INCOMPATIBLE STAFF

Underperforming team members cost your business a lot of money, and the problem may not simply be lack of ability. You may have team members who do not agree with your business philosophy and thinking. They may not agree with the way you run your business, or how your prices are structured. Honestly, they may think you're an idiot, but you pay their wage so they put up with it.

Many years ago I had an employee, and unbeknown to me he didn't believe in a particular system I had implemented. At the time my business was really busy and I was only focusing on the monthly turnover, I wasn't looking at individual performance. However, after attending a weekend workshop I began paying a little more attention to my business. Only then did I notice he was not performing very well in a particular area. When I spoke with him and asked why, he told me he thought my system was rubbish and refused to implement it as part of our sales process. It seriously made no sense, but based on that I had to let him go.

If KPIs had been in place and measured weekly, I would have identified this problem within a matter of weeks and saved my business a lot of money. I estimate he lost me approximately $40,000 in revenue over a nine-month period, but it could have been much worse. *This is why knowing the numbers is important.*

WHAT'S THE DIFFERENCE BETWEEN STATISTICS AND KPIs?

Basically, statistics look at the past – *where you've been* – whereas KPIs look at the present – *where you are right now. KPIs are looking at today, this week and this month.* Because KPIs show current, up-to-date information, you can use these numbers to verify if your business is on track to achieve a particular weekly or monthly target. KPIs also give you the ability to make sudden changes within your business that will have a direct influence on tomorrow and therefore this week's figures.

Statistics, on the other hand, have no influence on the future as they only show what has already happened – what you've already achieved or not achieved. Statistics only give you an idea of what may occur in the future; they cannot be used to instigate change.

For example, you may have a goal to see 80 new clients this month. You've implemented certain strategies and have a great marketing campaign in place, which you're closely monitoring. Obviously you feel this goal is achievable, because *statistics show* that for the same period last year you saw 70 new clients, so 80 new clients is a stretch but it's well within reach; however, knowing this past statistical figure will have no influence on achieving this month's target of 80 new clients.

As the weeks progress, your weekly KPIs will keep you informed as to whether you will or will not achieve your target of 80 new clients for the month. If your weekly KPIs show you're falling short of your goal, you can start making changes immediately. These changes can be monitored and further changes made if required, or individual team training implemented as needed. This is the power of having KPIs in place.

> **"If you can't measure it, you can't improve it."**
>
> Peter Drucker

It's no secret…there's money in small business, however you need to know your daily, weekly and monthly numbers.

After reading this chapter, what ideas are going through your head? Write them down *right now*.

_____

_____

_____

_____

_____

_____

_____

THE THREE WAYS TO INCREASE TURNOVER AND PROFITS

Everything you've read so far is important and necessary if you want to own a successful business, but in it's most simplistic form increasing your business turnover and having greater profits involves three basic areas of improvement:

- *Attracting more new clients:*
  - Better marketing
  - Smarter marketing
  - More effective marketing
  - Targeted marketing
- *Getting your new clients to spend more money each time they visit your business:*
  - Offering additional retail options
  - Increasing the types of services you offer

- – Internal marketing – make sure your clients know what you do

- – Increasing your prices

■ *Getting your new and existing clients to return to your business more often:*

- – Recommend further services

- – Follow up missed quotes and opportunities

- – Increase your client contact methods

No matter how you look at it, it's that simple.

Let's look at an example to demonstrate how a small change in each of these three areas of your business can produce outstanding results. Let's assume the next 10 new clients that enter your business spend $100 per visit. This would equate to $1000 in gross turnover. If all 10 clients visit your business three times over the next 12 months then your annual turnover would be $3000 from these 10 clients.

Now, if you worked a little smarter on all three areas of your business and you managed to increase each area by only 10%, this would equate to 11 new clients instead of 10, and they would spend $110 per visit instead of $100, and they would return to your business 3.3 times per year instead of only three times.

Let's look at the numbers: 11 new clients × $110 × 3.3 visits per client = $3993, which is a $993 increase in turnover, or 33%, which is good. If you use the same formula but increase all three areas by 20%, it gets even more exciting: 12 new clients × $120 × 3.6 visits per client = $5184, which is a massive $2184 increase in turnover, or 72.8%, which is great.

As you can see, a small change in all three areas of your business produces outstanding results because of the compounding effect. A common mistake with business owners is their lack of attention on all three areas of their business. Yes, you do need to attract new clients to your business, but if this is your only area of focus you're going to have to work so much harder to produce the same results.

Once again, *numbers don't lie*: to achieve a $2184 improvement by just increasing new client numbers and neglecting the other two areas, you would have to attract 17 new clients instead of 10, which equates to a massive 70% increase. Trying to increase your new clients by 70% each and every month is going to be hard work, and believe me, this is how I used to run my own business. All my focus and attention was on new clients, but once I realised I could work smarter by working on small incremental increases in all three areas of my business, I produced better results with much less work on a more consistent basis.

INCREASING YOUR PRICES

Many business owners put off increasing their prices because they're concerned clients will get angry and go somewhere else. Here's the truth of the matter: if you're not getting 10% of your clients complaining about your prices then you're too cheap, and only C and D clients will eventually leave because receiving a quality service is not important to them, only price is. However, your A and B clients will stay if they feel your prices are justified. My accountant is not cheap, and I know that I could find a cheaper accountant by making a few phone calls, but I've stayed with him because he provides excellent service. If I have an urgent matter I can call his mobile and he always answers it, and that's exactly what I need in an accountant. It makes me feel someone has got my back, and yes I know I pay for it.

A few years ago a friend of mine purchased a business in Brisbane from someone retiring. It was a very profitable business, even though their prices were quite low. This business also had a very large percentage of elderly clientele, which was not their target market, so the new owner decided to put the prices up by 20% on all services, thinking this would make many of the elderly clients go elsewhere, and in return the increased prices would balance the total loss of clients; however, it backfired and the business got busier.

What the new owner failed to realise was that when they increased their prices many clients perceived that they must have been more experienced and were offering a better service, and so they paid the new prices, and they also referred their friends and family, resulting in a $100,000 per year increase in revenue, which makes me wonder how much money the previous owner let slip through their fingers, leading up to retirement. Yes, a few clients did go elsewhere, but as you can probably guess, they were the C and D clients. So not only did the new owner make a lot more money, they also got a better list of clients by removing the blowflies.

Don't make the same mistake yourself. Don't simply charge the same price as everyone else if you feel you offer more and provide a far better service. Be like my accountant: his prices match his service.

Think of all the different businesses you currently interact with on a regular basis and consider why you continue to work with them. How many of them are using the three compounding methods described above? Most probably are. Was it their initial marketing campaign that attracted you in the first place? Are they always in contact with you, keeping you informed about new products and services? Have they increased their prices, but you still choose them over their competitors? If you look at all the reasons why you work with this particular business, you've got to remember your clients are no different.

It's no secret…there's money in small business, however you must understand the concept of compounding.

After reading this chapter, what ideas are going through your head?
Write them down *right now*.

_____

_____

_____

_____

_____

_____

_____

_____

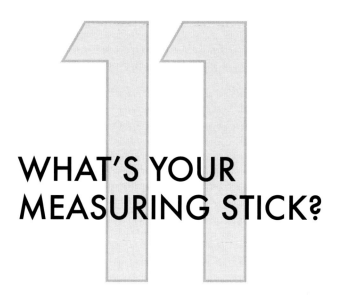

WHAT'S YOUR
MEASURING STICK?

Before moving into systems and marketing, I thought I would touch on a concept I've been using for years. It drives my wife nuts at times, but it serves me very well – I call it *The Orthotic Economy*, and it's my personal and business measuring stick for working out what I will and will not invest in.

Now, if you're a Lawyer you can call it *The Will Economy*, if you're a Hairdresser you can call it *The Style, Cut & Colour Economy*, or if you're a Real Estate Salesperson you can call it *The House Sale Economy* – your profession, industry or trade is irrelevant because this concept works for everyone, but only if you're willing to open your mind. *(If you do not know what an orthotic is, it's a shoe insert that podiatrists make to support the arch of the foot – that's the simple explanation.)*

This is how it works: there's an event or business training seminar being held interstate and you really want to attend but you're deciding if you should or should not go because of the costs involved. Let's say it will cost you $3000, by the time you pay for your ticket to attend, accommodation, airfares and food. Now you're thinking, *this is a lot of money to attend an event, there's no way I'm paying that.* However, here's how The Orthotic Economy works, because I'm using orthotics as a simple measuring stick.

If the fee for an orthotic is $500, how many orthotics would I need to make to pay for the conference? At $500, I would only need to make an extra six pairs of orthotics to pay for the whole trip (6 × $500 = $3000), which is realistic. This may seem like a strange economic formula, but it does put things into perspective, and believe me it works. It's only six pairs of orthotics, and if I attend the event with that mindset I may learn something that allows me to make an extra six pairs of orthotics per month, every month, making an additional $36,000 per year. If this was the case the initial $3000 investment would now seem insignificant. After ten years it would equate to $360,000 – which is a nice return.

If you're a Lawyer, how much do you charge to create a will for someone? My wife and I recently had our wills redrawn, and I wish it only cost the same as an orthotic. So if an event cost $3000, or maybe $8000, how many wills do you need to draw up to get your investment back? Did you notice I said "investment", because every time you spend money on your own self-development or education … it's an investment, not an expense.

Every business and profession has a product or a service that can be used as their measuring stick. In podiatry it's an orthotic, but what's yours? Think about it. If you own a shop and you sell multiple small items, no big ticket items, you may need to group a few together.

Have you ever considered having a one-on-one business coach? It may cost you $1000, $1500, or maybe even $2500 per month based on the service they provide, and I've heard many business owners say that those sorts of figures are utterly ridiculous. However, it's only two, three or five pairs of orthotics per month if you use The Orthotic Economy. I first used a business coach myself 15 years ago and their fee at that time was $1000 per month, which was two orthotics, so I thought if I can make an extra two orthotics per month using their advice then it's not costing me anything…it's *free*. The end result was I made an extra 30 pairs per month and made an additional $15,000 per month, or $180,000 for that year, and it kept going upwards. Once again The Orthotic Economy served me well.

"If you change the way you look at things, the things you look at change."

Wayne Dyer

I use The Orthotic Economy in all areas of my life, not just at work. I recently bought a Gorilla costume – as you do – and it was $389, and I thought immediately, *that's less than one orthotic*, so I purchased it. When I go out for dinner with my wife and I look at the final bill, I don't see $125, I see a quarter of an orthotic.

This doesn't mean that I recommend splashing money around like there's no tomorrow, what I'm suggesting is that you should use The Orthotic Economy, The Will Economy, The Cut, Colour & Style Economy or The House Sale Economy as a measuring stick to help you make intelligent, informed business decisions. Don't look at a piece of equipment and think it will cost $5000, instead it really only costs ten orthotics, three wills, or maybe one house sale. Once you've mastered it at work, start applying this concept to all areas of your life.

After reading this chapter, what ideas are going through your head? Write them down *right now*.

_____

_____

_____

_____

_____

_____

_____

_____

SYSTEMS

Businesses that fail to have systems also fail to reach their full potential, because you cannot run a successful business by hoping everyone is doing a particular task correctly. Some businesses have "informal" systems, but a system not documented is also a system for failure. If you do not develop written systems, a set of guidelines for your team to follow, your team will just start making them up as they go and this causes confusion between team members and ultimately poor results.

SEVEN REASONS WHY YOU SHOULD DEVELOP SYSTEMS

1   *Improved productivity:* Everyone involved in the business will have a set of processes to follow which will deliver a predictable result each and every time it is followed correctly, which will improve productivity and develop a happier work environment.

2   *Greater client satisfaction and confidence:* This results in higher profits and return business. You will receive more referrals from clients who are satisfied with your service and have confidence in your advice. When clients refer friends and family and you do a great job, it makes them look good as well.

3   *Fewer mistakes and errors:* With systems in place there is greater control over how information is distributed throughout the business, which results in less double-handling and reduces errors. There's also less guessing.

4   *Better accountability for team members:* If an error does occur, well-documented systems will allow you to identify the point at which the error occurred and who may be responsible for the error.

5   *Less reliance on the business owner:* Systems give the business owner freedom. A good system should document the question, the answer and the expected outcome, so team members can make decisions without the business owner being present.

6   *Improved training:* It is much easier to train new team members when systems are in place. Even the training process itself can be a system.

In my business I had a 20-day training program in place for all new team members. I had a checklist that I followed, which listed activities and duties that must be achieved within a particular timeframe. As each task was achieved I ticked it off the list. New and current team members were unaware this system existed – but it was a very important system for me as the business owner. You need to develop this.

7   *Consistency:* I believe this to be the most important reason for having formalised and well-developed business systems. Your clients will notice consistency, and when tasks are completed in a consistent manner it speeds up the process.

THE IMPORTANCE OF CONSISTENCY

Consistency means being reliable and dependable and maintaining a constant profile and level of service. *Consistency* may not always be noticed, but *inconsistency* will be noticed every time. *Consistency* is about being *"the best you can be"* on a consistent basis. It's not about trying to copy someone else's level of service that you cannot possibly replicate.

Being consistent doesn't mean you have to be outstanding.

"Hang on, hang on, why can't we be outstanding?"

Well, you can be outstanding if you want, as long as you can be outstanding on a consistent basis. But if you think about it, if you can be outstanding every day, without compromise or error, then this is really your level of consistency, because it is *"the best you can be"*. If you cannot be outstanding on a consistent basis, you need to dial it down a notch and be *"the best you can be"* on a consistent basis. I would much rather receive a consistent above-average service from a business every time I visited them than receive awesome service one day and poor service the next. When you're treated poorly after being treated well, you notice it – and so will your clients. I've visited businesses and have been offered a coffee on the first and fourth visits, but not offered coffee on the second, third and fifth visits, and yes I noticed it. In contrast, I've been to other businesses that have never offered me a coffee, and funnily enough I don't expect it, but the rest of their service is consistent. So clients will notice inconsistency, however they won't tell you directly how much it annoys them, but they will tell other people.

PEOPLE FOLLOW SYSTEMS; SYSTEMS SHOULD NEVER FOLLOW PEOPLE

Having systems takes away the guesswork and allows everyone to concentrate fully on client needs, not their own needs. When developing systems, never change them to suit one person. If a task requires everyone to do three steps, but you have one person in your team who says they do not like doing step 2 because *"it just doesn't suit them"*, do not change the system to suit that one person unless they can show you a valid reason why the system should be changed.

If it is a valid reason then you could modify the system and create a new system for everyone in the business to follow. This is why employing new people can be fun and rewarding: you're getting fresh new eyes, and sometimes systems do become outdated and need to be shaken up. Also, new team members who have worked elsewhere may have observed some systems that are better than the ones you currently have in place, so you must be open to their positive suggestions.

However – and I can't stress point this enough – when a new person joins your team, tell them you want their input, suggestions and ideas on how existing systems and processes can be improved upon, but they cannot come to you with these changes until they have worked in your business for a full six months. The reason you want them to wait a full six months is because you want them to see how the whole system works over a given timeframe, not just one small snippet of the system that they've been exposed to in the first week or month. *My friend, Dave M. Frees, a Lawyer and Trust Attorney in Pennsylvania, says this point is so important he puts it in their employment contract, because if you don't, they will have a tendency to come to you every week telling you what needs to be changed, without seeing the full picture.*

ELIMINATING BAD HABITS

You should be aware though that some team members who have worked elsewhere could bring with them some bad habits, which could be in direct conflict with the systems you are trying to introduce or teach. But the good news is *systems eliminate bad habits.*

Some bad habits will be the direct result of working somewhere with no systems. However, some people are just lazy, have no work ethic, and will always take the easy road, so their habits have nothing to do with previous employment but more to do with their attitude towards work. Don't let them fool you into believing that their bad habits are a valid reason to change your current system. This is often identified with constant comments such as, *"At the last place I worked we used to…".*

If a team member brings an idea to you, listen and then decide if it's worth considering, and tell them you will bring it up at the next meeting for further discussion so you can get opinions from other team members. Doing this shows you are open to change and willing to listen, but you will take a team approach to introduction or rejection of new ideas. This way, if everyone thinks it is a bad idea you can shoot it down as a group, but the person who made the suggestion will still feel they have been listened to.

YOUR SYSTEMS SHOULD BE SEEN AND NOT JUST HEARD

Every business will have systems to some extent, but usually they are not written down and instead are taught by word of mouth. Learning by repetition and continual re-training can work well as long as the business owner or senior team members are always prepared to make themselves available to answer ongoing and repetitive questions, which is not what you want. A better way is to have all your systems in written format in a set of handbooks and flowcharts to explain the processes.

SYSTEMS AND SUB-SYSTEMS

Every task within your business should have a written system, and the more technical systems will need to have sub-systems created for easier management. All written systems should fit onto one sheet of paper; if it goes longer than this, it's an indication you need sub-systems.

For example, you may have a system titled *Telephone Usage System*, however in its entirety it would be a huge system to learn, with many pages, so it's better managed and easier to teach if it is broken into sub-systems. Below are examples of sub-systems that could be created from the *Telephone Usage System*.

Sub-system: "How to answer the telephone"

- How many rings are acceptable before the telephone should be answered?

- How should the telephone be answered? I get annoyed when the phone is answered, the person politely says the company name and then ends with saying, "This is Mary speaking". Ahhh! Well of course you're speaking Mary, otherwise I would not be able to hear you. If you have team members saying this, please stop them. All they need to say is, "this is Mary".

- Everyone should be saying the same phrase and following a "script".

- The exact wording of the "script" forms part of your system.

Sub-system: "Identifying client enquiries"

- What questions should be asked to identify a new or existing client's needs?

Sub-system: "Common questions clients ask over the telephone"

- If you asked the person who answers your phone to write down all the questions they receive over a week, you'll find many questions are quite repetitive; therefore you should have scripted answers for these commonly asked questions.

The telephone is one of the most powerful tools in your business, and it can make you a lot of money if it is used correctly, however if used poorly it can also lose you a lot of money.

IDENTIFYING POOR PERFORMERS

Without systems, team members have an excuse for making ongoing errors. They can easily say they forgot how to do something, or tell you they got busy and overlooked a particular task. Having documented systems in place will eliminate this and also help you identify team members that should not be working in your business.

HOW DO YOU KNOW WHEN YOUR SYSTEMS ARE WORKING?

It's easy to know if your systems are working because your whole business runs without any interruptions. There's no client complaints, no arguments between team members and no bottlenecks or delays. There is complete harmony in the workplace. Another good sign everything is working well is that you can go on holidays for a few weeks and nothing has changed when you return, except your tan and your weight.

However, even when everything is running well, it's still a good idea to test your systems. Occasionally ask team members to explain a particular system to you. Are they still doing it the same as it is documented, or have they gone off track slightly? *Is there a reason for going off track?* If so, review your written document to see if something needs further development or if the team needs re-training. People can move away from a system without even knowing it, especially when it happens slowly. This is why system reviews are essential – especially when things are going well.

> **"A good system shortens the road to the goal."**
>
> Orison Swett Marden

WRITE SYSTEMS FOR 12 YEAR OLDS

As adults we like to complicate simple tasks so that they seem far more important than they really are, and systems are no different.

They do not need to be overly complicated to be effective. In fact, if a system is really good any 12 year old should be able to read it and implement it without any real concerns.

The hardest part about creating a system is getting started. So to help you out, here is my Four-Step Formula for creating effective systems:

Step 1: Write down how things are done in your business. This may sound very simple, but many business owners never get this far and instead they keep everything in their head.

Step 2: Implement the system, meaning have someone follow your instructions to see if it actually works and makes sense.

Step 3: Review the outcome and evaluate the system's effectiveness – then the final step…

Step 4: Rewrite the system.

You should also be reviewing your systems on a regular basis because systems are not static, they are dynamic and should continually be revised.

A common question I've been asked is, *"Why do I need to write something down when it's pretty obvious how it should be done?"* Thinking this way is a common mistake; the more obvious a system seems, the more reason it needs to be written down.

As an example:

How do you make a cup of instant coffee?

1   Put coffee in cup.

2   Add sugar.

3   Add boiling water.

4   Add milk.

This is a very straightforward system, but because it is so simple it is open to interpretation and can result in some good and bad cups of coffee. Now, what would happen if you asked your 12-year-old son to make you a cup of coffee for you based on the above instructions; how would he go? He would start off with enthusiasm, but then constantly interrupt you for further clarification about the instructions he's been given because it's not clear:

1   How much coffee do you have? Would you prefer a heaped or level spoonful? I noticed there are two different spoons in the drawer – which one would you like me to use?

2   Would you prefer a cup or a mug? Which size mug? I noticed there is a mug that has *"I work with Idiots"* printed on the side – is this your mug?

3   How many sugars did you want? Sorry, but did you mean heaped or level? I just noticed there are sugar pills – are these

yours? *Are you a diabetic? Is there a family history of diabetes? Should I be concerned?*

4   Okay, you're not a diabetic, but how much milk would you like?

5   What type of milk? I've noticed you have full cream, low fat, no fat, skim and lactose-free milk in the fridge. *That's a lot of milk. Are you lactose intolerant? I get a lot of wind myself after drinking milk.*

Now this may sound ridiculous, but if you don't have written systems for team members to follow, you will constantly be interrupted throughout the day with meaningless questions, not that much different to a 12 year old asking, *"What milk do you want?"* Are you finding this happens to you already, every single day? Is it affecting your own productivity and driving you nuts yet?

A few years ago I had a problem in my own business when it came to sterilising instruments for nail surgery. New team members found it difficult to remember which instruments needed to be bagged together, even though *I thought it was pretty obvious.* After numerous attempts at trying to rewrite the system, explaining what each instrument looked like and what size bag was needed so there were no further errors, one of the team said, "why don't we just take photographs of the instruments that should be grouped together and also what size bag should be used?" So this is exactly what we did, and these photos were laminated and placed on the wall next to the sterilisation machine. From that point onwards there was not another error.

"A bad system will beat a good person every time."

W. Edwards Deming

DEVELOPING YOUR SYSTEMS

So how do you get started writing systems? The easiest way is to just hand write them. It may not be perfect, but this is better than not having them documented at all. You can always have someone type your notes up for you at a later date and make it look good. What matters most is that you get something down on paper for your team to follow, especially if you have nothing documented right now.

Once your systems are documented and the people involved in performing these tasks get a chance to evaluate and apply them exactly as they have been explained, only then will holes become apparent. When holes are identified you patch them up as you go, however if there are too many holes you may need to throw the system out altogether and develop a new system from scratch. This is how systems develop, and sometimes you just need to know when a system is no good and when it is time to start again. Even though developing systems takes time and effort, it should be something that is ever evolving within your business.

Use your smartphone

Another easy way to start documenting your systems is to use a voice recorder. Everyone has a smartphone these days, so pick it up, hit record, and start talking about how you do a particular task or process. When it's done, give the recording to someone and have them type it for you, if you want a written or electronic systems manual. However, there's no reason why a system cannot be an audio file. If you're going to use this method, I would suggest investing in a lapel microphone for better sound quality. *I personally use a Rode lapel mic.*

You may also use your smartphone to take photos and shoot videos to explain a system, especially if it's difficult to explain in writing. Pictures are great, and the saying *a picture says a thousand words* is correct. Shooting video is an awesome way to explain a system, but once again invest in a lapel microphone for better quality sound. And if you're going to go to all the trouble of recording audio and video, I would suggest having a basic script outlining the key points you want to cover, as you don't want to come across as disjointed.

Your systems may eventually be a combination of written manuals (hard copy and electronic), photographs, audio recordings (online and offline) and instructional videos. You're only limited by your imagination.

SYSTEMS ADD VALUE

A business with good systems will sell for more than a business without systems. It will also be easier to sell because the new owners can clearly see how things are done because they're documented. My business sold for a healthy seven-figure amount because the buyers wanted my business systems and they understood the value of good systems.

Your business systems form part of your intellectual property and therefore should be protected. Only the business owner should have access to all systems; other team members only need to have access to systems that are required for their particular duties.

Never leave all your systems in one place, accessible to everyone. How would you feel if a copy of all your business systems was given to your opposition? This can happen if a team member leaves your employment and sets up in opposition to you, so you need to protect your intellectual property. Everyone should be made aware that no parts of your system manuals should be copied or taken home without permission.

SYSTEM OVERLAP

As you develop systems you will notice that where one system ends, another one begins. This leads to systems overlapping, which is why some systems will be duplicated in different system manuals, because more than one person is involved in completing a particular task. When you have multiple team members looking after different areas of your business you must have systems in place to make sure they are communicating with one another correctly.

Your method of communication is a big system overlap between all team members. I learnt this the hard way. A few years ago my marketing assistant and I came up with an idea to promote a new piece of equipment I had purchased, and without telling anyone else in the business we placed an ad in the weekend newspaper. Sounds harmless so far … what could possibly go wrong? In my advertising I explained all the benefits and why it was something everyone needed.

I was very happy with my strategy, but I made two mistakes. Firstly, I forgot to tell my receptionists about the upcoming ad, and secondly, I didn't realise not all of my reception team had been trained about the new equipment. As expected, the telephone went nuts with enquiries, and my Receptionists couldn't understand why the sudden interest in this new equipment, which they knew nothing about. Needless to say, my nomination for boss of the year went out the window, but more importantly my business reputation could have been damaged. Fortunately it wasn't, but it pointed out a huge flaw in my systems: my overlapping systems of how each person communicated with each other.

The larger the business, the more areas of system overlap.

It's no secret…there's money in small business, however you must have systems in place and they must be followed by everyone.

After reading this chapter, what ideas are going through your head?
Write them down *right now*.

_____

_____

_____

_____

_____

_____

_____

WORKING ON THE
BUSINESS

When your systems are well documented and delegated to the appropriate people it's time for you to start moving onto more important functions within the business. This is referred to as *"working on the business"* instead of *"working in the business"*. This doesn't mean that you have to stop doing what you love, it just means modifying your day and stepping back a little.

Working *on*, instead of *in*, your business means you start focusing on the areas of your business that will contribute to long-term growth and expansion, but it doesn't mean that you "have to" do these things. The best thing about working for yourself and being the business owner is that you get to choose what you do, or don't do. Therefore working on your business is a choice. Some business owners prefer to stay small, but having said that, if you want to sustain a financially successful business for yourself and your family, you need to spend adequate time working on the business and not just in it.

A lot of business owners spend eight hours a day, or more, with clients, then neglect their families for a few more hours because they do not have tasks delegated to their support team. You cannot continue to do this long term without it affecting your health or your relationships.

For those of you who want to have a bigger business and one day have multiple locations, working *on your business* instead of *in your business* is something you must do. *You do not have the choice.* It doesn't mean you have to give up working with clients altogether, but your contact time will definitely need to be reduced if expansion and multiple locations are a long-term goal.

You need to work out what works best for you. You have to find your balance between management tasks, business growth and client contact. For some, giving up complete client contact works very well, while others need to stay in touch with their clients, even if only a few days per month. Once again, it's all about choice and what you want to achieve.

SO WHAT IS INVOLVED WHEN YOU WORK ON THE BUSINESS?

Working on your business involves more mental energy than physical energy and involves you paying more attention to areas within the business that are often overlooked and neglected, such as:

- Financial planning – it's easy to overlook your finances, especially when you're busy. More money coming in than going out is not the best financial planning method to use.

- Expansion planning – are you thinking of opening more locations, or are you thinking of expanding the size of your current location? Is it time to renovate?

- Identifying marketing opportunities – you see more opportunities when your mind is free from clutter. Working with clients for eight or more hours every day is mentally tiring and leaves you with no headspace for creativity. You miss opportunities when you're tired.

- Team development – spending time developing your team will pay dividends.

- Strategic development – what strategies do you have in place to develop your business further? With more free time you can further develop your business relationships.

- Innovative development – are you always going to do things the way you currently do them? What other cool software, apps or equipment can you introduce?

- Further system development – there is nothing wrong with constantly developing your systems, but don't introduce a minor change every week or your team will start to get confused. Allow time between system changes so you can test and measure their effectiveness.

- Networking – with more time available, you should become more involved in networking opportunities in your area.

Working on your business is not an easy habit to create, especially if you've not done it before. To do it effectively you need to block out time in your diary and you need to commit to it. This is one activity where I would really suggest you get yourself a business coach because it is so easy to take an afternoon off to work on your business, and instead you end up doing something else. You need to be held accountable to someone other than yourself, and it needs to be on a regular basis.

A business coach can help you with understanding the effectiveness of time blocking and other time management strategies. I'm yet to see anyone successfully work on their business without getting guidance from someone else. It sounds easy to do, but it's difficult to implement without accountability.

After reading this chapter, what ideas are going through your head?
Write them down *right now.*

_____

_____

_____

_____

_____

_____

_____

ARE YOU GREEN AND GROWING OR RIPE AND ROTTING?

To learn more about systems I would highly recommend reading *The E-Myth Revisited* by Michael Gerber, and anything written about Ray Kroc, the man behind the success of McDonald's. Ray Kroc was once asked why McDonald's was such a phenomenal success, and his answer was very simple: *"We take the hamburger business more serious than anyone else making hamburgers"*, and he was probably right.

How seriously do you take your own business? Did you set it up because it was better than working for someone else? Are you willing to do what is required to make it a successful enterprise?

The worldwide success of McDonald's came about by having amazing yet very simple systems. Systems don't need to be complicated to be successful; they just need to have three ingredients:

- They need to be followed by everyone in the business.

- They need to be developed further as the business landscape changes.

- They need to be documented.

Could you imagine McDonald's if Ray Kroc had never spent the time documenting how a cheeseburger should be made? Ray Kroc's McDonald's is run on systems that are so simple; he has been able to create a billion-dollar business basically run by kids. These kids can't clean their bedrooms at home and many don't even have a driver's licence, however they are an integral part of a billion-dollar burger empire. Understanding the power of systems will make you money.

"Are you green and growing or ripe and rotting?"

Ray Kroc

Your greatest growth period in business occurs when you're green, when everything is new and exciting. The problem though is when you stop growing, when you become complacent, settled and happy with what you've achieved. *You've become ripe.* If you don't re-invent yourself and replant new business ideas or change the way you do things within your business, it will slowly begin to rot *and smell.*

When a business becomes ripe, the business owner has three options:

1   Do nothing and eventually rot – this is a poor option, but is not uncommon.

2   Introduce new services and equipment and improve upon the successful formula they already have in place and working.

3   Expand and open multiple locations.

Options 2 and 3 are both good.

It's no secret…there's money in small business, however you need to have systems in place and they need to be working well.

After reading this chapter, what ideas are going through your head? Write them down *right now.*

_____

_____

_____

_____

_____

_____

_____

_____

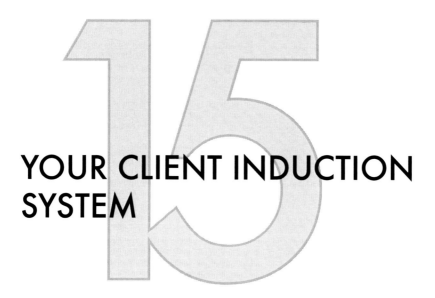

YOUR CLIENT INDUCTION SYSTEM

The aim of having an *induction system* is to ensure that first-time users of your business are greeted correctly and consistently when they arrive, and the key is consistency, which I have mentioned numerous times. When a client arrives at our business it is important to acknowledge them immediately. It doesn't matter how busy everyone is, it's not difficult to give someone a simple smile to acknowledge his or her presence. There's nothing worse than arriving somewhere and the person at the front counter continues to talk on the telephone and does not acknowledge your existence. When you're left hanging, sixty seconds can seem like an eternity.

I'm one of those people who gets annoyed quickly when I'm ignored and treated poorly. As far as I'm concerned it says they do not care about me.

What message do you want your clients to receive when they arrive at your business?

Your client induction system is more than just a greeting. If it was just about greeting a client, this would be called your client greeting system, but it's not. Your client induction system is about creating a positive, lasting impression, which is what you want your clients to take away with them when they leave your business.

If your business uses an induction form for new clients, make sure it is completed fully by each client, and enquire if you cannot understand their handwriting or if the spelling looks a little odd. It's better to ask straight away while the client is in front of you rather than trying to phone them later on. With today's technology you may find the client has already supplied most of their information online.

If a client refuses to give you all their information, this is your first indication that you may be dealing with a C or D type client.

Here's how simple your client induction system can be:

- Client arrives: make sure you greet them with a smile.

- If you're busy with another person or you're on the telephone, always acknowledge their presence.

- Have them complete your client induction sheet if this information has not already been obtained.

- If your business runs by appointments, let them know immediately if there's going to be a delay, and keep them updated with their waiting time.

- Offer them a coffee, tea or glass of water while they wait. How simple is that, yet it's often overlooked.

- If the client wants to talk and if you do not have other clients to deal with, talk with them. This is far more important than shuffling paperwork and it builds good long-term rapport.

- Finally, never discuss personal issues with other team members at the front counter.

Does this induction system seem difficult to follow? No, it doesn't. But if it's so simple why do so many businesses get it wrong?

Do they not care, or has the business owner simply neglected to write an induction system for the team to follow?

When a client visits your business for the first time, or when an existing client returns, you want it to be a positive experience, therefore your business should always be bright and inviting, floors should be always be clean, magazines should be up to date and the overall layout of the business should look organised and uncluttered. Sometimes it's the simplest things that leave a lasting impression and make clients talk about your business long after their visit. Once a week, you should step out of the confines of your office and sit in your waiting area or foyer, or walk the floor of your business and look at things from a client's perspective. If you have waiting chairs, sit in each waiting chair and look around. You will be surprised what you can see, which is often overlooked by the rest of your team who work on the other side of the front counter.

"It's kind of fun to do the impossible."

Walt Disney

You and your team should be constantly looking for ways to "wow" both your new and existing clients when they enter your business, and it should be part of your overall induction system. Think of other businesses that have wowed the pants off you. What did they do? Was it complicated, and can you do something similar?

In 2012 I visited Disneyland with my wife and daughter and we had an awesome time, and when it comes to being wowed I don't think too many businesses do it better than Disney. It is the happiest place on earth. Now if you've been to Disneyland you may agree or disagree with my comments, but the one thing that you cannot deny is that the Disney Corporation is constantly looking for ways to wow their visitors when they enter their parks. Their *wow* is a part of their induction system – what's yours?

It's no secret…there's money in small business, however you need to wow your clients.

After reading this chapter, what ideas are going through your head? Write them down *right now*.

_____

_____

_____

_____

_____

_____

_____

_____

PART II
MARKETING

UNDERSTANDING THE BASICS OF MARKETING

Here's the simple truth of marketing: without it your business will fail. Marketing is what distinguishes you from your competitors and it relays a message to your target markets. As a business owner you should constantly be in marketing mode, not just some of the time, but all of the time, and you should be looking for new opportunities, because business success comes to those that search for it. Internet and social media have changed the way we communicate, think, and access information, however regardless of these online advancements some fundamentals of marketing have remained unchanged.

TIME AND PLACE

Is there a perfect time or perfect place to market your business? You better believe there is, and it's *anytime* and *anyplace*. Opportunities to market your business are everywhere; you just need to keep an open mind and never limit your search to your own profession or industry; instead, look at the broader market: your hairdresser and the coffee shop across the road, what are they doing that captures your attention? Have you seen another business use a marketing campaign and wondered if that could also work for your business? If so, borrow their idea and make it your own.

My local hairdresser, Jan Lyons Salon, offers free wi-fi, which is not unusual these days. But she also offers iPads for those who don't have a device with them, in case clients want to check emails or surf the web while they wait. Children can also use the iPads while their parents are having a haircut. Offering free wi-fi and use of iPads is an inexpensive idea, yet very effective and memorable – but will you implement this idea yourself?

CONSISTENCY AND SIMPLICITY IN YOUR MARKETING MESSAGE

Regardless of how you market your business, the most important thing is the *consistency and simplicity* in your marketing message. You will do far better marketing one message at a time and only to the target markets you want to attract. When you think McDonald's, you think hamburgers, because that's the message they've pushed since 1955. But everyone knows they also sell fries, hot apple pies and soft drinks, but they rarely mention this, unless they're promoting an upgrade meal deal or a special promotion.

If you want to see more of a particular type of client or sell more of a particular product, then push that one simple message and push it on a consistent basis, just like McDonald's hamburgers. Now this doesn't mean you will never sell another product or see another type of client, but you only have a limited amount of time to capture your audience with your marketing message, and by keeping your message simple, consistent, focused, and straight to the point your marketing is going to be more effective and reliable. Also, if you want to make more money, make sure your marketing is targeted towards your services and/or products with the highest profit margins and greatest dollar yield per hour.

> *"Consistent action creates consistent results."*
>
> Christine Kane

HELICOPTER MARKETING

Many business owners make the mistake of only marketing their business when business is slow, and once business improves they stop all their marketing activities again. This is a very ineffective and inconsistent way to market your business as it destroys momentum. Every time your marketing comes to a complete stop, it takes far more time and energy to get a campaign started again, which is why this form of marketing is referred to as *helicopter marketing*. A helicopter burns far more fuel to get off the ground than it does once it is up and running smoothly through the air. Every time it lands and comes to a complete standstill, it has to once again burn more fuel to get back off the ground.

WHAT IS A MARKETING NICHE?

Earlier we discussed your ideal client and your perfect target market, or multiple markets, however what happens if your business provides a similar service or sells a similar product as your competitors? If you're all marketing the same message, how does a client or customer differentiate your business from your competitors? They can't, so you need to create a niche, something that sets your business apart from the competition.

Creating a niche is all about positioning your business in a particular spot within an existing market. For example, all accounting firms do taxation, however what if an Accountant advertised that they specialised in tax minimisation for Hairdressers. This doesn't mean they cannot do taxation for other industries, but creating a niche in an area that's different to every other accounting firm starts to set them apart from the crowd.

If you constantly repeat this message you will be perceived as the expert in that niche, and if I were a Hairdresser I would visit you over your competitors.

WHOEVER CREATES THE NICHE FIRST, OWNS THE NICHE

To further cement the hairdresser niche the Accountant would visit every hairdresser in their area and meet the business owners, informing them of their expertise in taxation for hairdressers. They would visit hairdressing suppliers and even attend hairdressing expos and competitions. They could donate a prize or an award. They need to hang out where hairdressers hang out. Over time they will slowly start to own that niche, and be known as the hairdressing accountant, and whoever creates the niche first, owns the niche.

> "Commit to a niche; try to stop being everything to everyone."
>
> Andrew Davis

Can you see how easy it is to dominate a specific market and create a niche for your business? And best of all, you don't actually have to have any personal experience in that particular niche; *it's pure perception, but perception is reality*. Your skill and expertise will grow with each client you successfully work with.

What happens if someone already owns the niche you want? If this happens, create a sub-niche. If a business has already become a guru in an area that you wanted to get involved in, you simply dig further than they have. For example, if an accounting firm already targets hairdressers, the new accountant may focus on hairdressers between the ages of 30 and 55 who have more than two employees. Your only limiting factor when it comes to developing target markets, a niche and sub-niches is your imagination.

WHAT ARE YOUR CLIENTS BUYING AND WHAT ARE YOU SELLING?

The general purpose of marketing is to attract new clients to your business, however before you can implement a successful marketing campaign you must first understand what it is your clients are buying and what it is that you are selling. Are you selling what your clients want to buy or are you trying to sell them something they don't want? Many business owners mistakenly think they are selling a service or a product to their clients, however this is wrong. Clients don't come to your business to buy a service or product, they come to you because they're looking for a solution to a problem; therefore you should be marketing solutions and nothing more.

A security company is not selling alarm systems, they are selling peace of mind. A mattress company is not selling beds; they are selling a good night's sleep. So what are you *really* selling? Instead of being a salesperson, become a problem solver and help solve clients' problems.

"Don't find customers for your products,
find products for your customers."

Seth Godin (that's problem solving)

MARKETING IS AN INVESTMENT, NOT AN EXPENSE

When money is tight, the biggest mistake you can make is to cut your marketing budget. It may seem like the most logical thing to do, but it's a mistake. Business owners tend to look at marketing as an expense, instead of a long-term business investment. You should consider your marketing budget as a fixed cost, just like you would your rent and electricity. However, the amount you invest is not as important as *"the message"* you put out there and the *"consistency"* of when you do it.

As a general rule you should commit a percentage of your gross turnover to ongoing marketing. I have done this with every business I have owned and I continue to do so. Anyone who tells you marketing is too expensive and they cannot afford to do it is also telling you they should not be in business. Marketing is part of business, so accept it.

> "The man who stops advertising to save money is like the man who stops the clock to save time."
>
> Thomas Jefferson

HOW MUCH ARE YOU PREPARED TO PAY FOR A NEW CLIENT?

If you think about it, when you advertise you are basically buying clients for your business, and your effectiveness in doing this will determine whether you're paying too much or getting them for a bargain. To calculate how much your new clients are costing you, you need to add up all your marketing for the year and divide this total figure by the total number of new clients for that year; this will give you your *new client acquisition cost,* and sometimes it will surprise you how much you pay.

For example, if you invested $30,000 in marketing in the previous financial year and your business saw 600 new clients in that same period, your *new client acquisition cost* would be approximately $50 per client. You must keep this figure in mind every time you're with a new client – remember that you just paid $50 to have them sit in front of you. *Were they worth it, or were they a blowfly?* If you have employees, you need to inform them about how much each client costs and they need to respect their value.

You will also come to learn that you may not make much money on a new client's first transaction. If your initial transaction was $100 and it cost you $50 to buy them, you've made a gross profit of $50. But this does not take into account rent and other running expenses, and if you have employees, well you're making very little – if anything – on a new client's first transaction. Your profits come from their next transaction and the one after that, and from their referrals. This is why every employee needs to understand the cost of a new client and the importance of good customer service, because this is what keeps them coming back.

It is far more cost effective to keep your existing clients coming back than it is to try to keep attracting new clients.

It's no secret...there's money in small business, however you must understand that marketing is an investment, not an expense.

After reading this chapter, what ideas are going through your head? Write them down *right now*.

_____

_____

_____

_____

_____

_____

_____

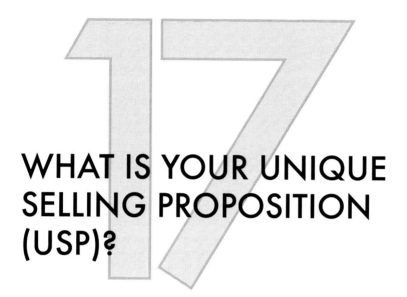

WHAT IS YOUR UNIQUE SELLING PROPOSITION (USP)?

This is really important to understand so read it slowly if you need to. Your *unique selling proposition,* better known as a USP, is a *short statement used in all your marketing to get a simple message about your business and the services it provides across to your potential clients in a matter of milliseconds.*

Does your business need to have a USP? Yes it does. A USP helps to differentiate your business from your competitors, and once you have developed your USP, you need to use it in all your marketing, not just some.

YOUR USP HAS TO BECOME SYNONYMOUS WITH YOUR BUSINESS

Your goal is to develop a strong USP so you stand out from the other businesses in your area that do not understand the power of a USP. As soon as a client sees your USP statement it portrays an important message about your business and lets them know what it is you do. This is especially important if you have a lot of competitors.

If you pay attention you will notice most larger businesses have a USP and they use it all the time. For example, M&M's *"Melts in your mouth, not in your hand"* is a very clear message. I remember when Smarties were the king of sugar-coated chocolate, but the problem was they used to melt in your hands if you held them too long. Then came along M&M's...they looked just like Smarties, but they didn't melt in your hands. When M&M's hit the market in the 1980s I cannot remember if they were cheaper or more expensive than Smarties, but I do remember their USP and I still eat them often, but I can't remember the last time I had Smarties.

If your USP is good and if it's used often enough in your marketing it will become memorable and will set your business apart from the crowd. It is important to remember when you develop a USP that your business must also be able to back it up, otherwise you are not telling the truth. Head & Shoulders cannot have a USP that says *"clinically proven to reduce dandruff"* if it doesn't reduce dandruff.

Most people still remember the USP used by FedEx: *"When it absolutely, positively has to be there overnight."* If you needed a package delivered overnight, you would more than likely think of FedEx first because of their strong USP.

YOUR USP SHOULD ALSO BE REVIEWED

Don't feel that once you have created a USP statement that you have to stick with it forever. Things change, other businesses catch up, and consumers may be looking for something different. Domino's Pizzas' USP used to be, *"You get fresh, hot pizza delivered to your door in 30 minutes or less, or it's free"*, but they stopped using this USP because of the perception of irresponsible driving, and modified it to *"You Got 30 Minutes"*, which still relates to it being delivered in 30 minutes, but there's no longer a guarantee. Regardless of the change, we all know Domino's delivers fast pizza. Your USP statement must change as your business develops, but don't change your USP unless you have something better to say.

HOW DO YOU DEVELOP A USP?

To develop a powerful USP for your business you need to bring together information you know about your business with what you think your target markets are looking for:

- What does your business do that no one else is currently doing?

- Can you improve or provide a service better than your competitors?

- Can you provide a faster service?

- Do you have a more specialised service (a niche)?

- Do you consistently run on time, which is important for busy people?

- Do you have better trading hours?

To make developing your USP easier, imagine you're the client – what are your needs and wants when you see a business similar to your own? Is running on time more important than price? For most of us time is money, so busy, hard-working people will pay a premium if you can consistently run on time. If time is not important, the client may complain about your prices because they are price driven. Can you see the difference? A client who is price driven would more than likely be attracted to a business with a USP containing the words "discount", "cheap" or "low cost".

In the next chapter we're going to develop your CPOD – your *competitive point of difference* – which is the final step towards developing your business "brand". When these last two pieces of the puzzle are put together you will be ready to start developing a marketing campaign that works and gets results. Many business owners want to take shortcuts and refuse to go through this preparation and development process of understanding their business fully, and then they wonder why their marketing campaigns fail. If you don't understand your business, how can you possibly expect your clients to understand your business?

> "Your Unique Selling Proposition must be relevant
> to your customers' needs, compelling enough to
> cause them to change, and most of all, true."
>
> Unknown

It's no secret…there's money in small business, however you must be prepared to do the groundwork.

After reading this chapter, what ideas are going through your head? Write them down *right now*.

_____

_____

_____

_____

_____

_____

_____

_____

WHAT'S YOUR COMPETITIVE POINT OF DIFFERENCE (CPOD)?

What is it that makes your business different from your competitors? You can say you're better than everyone else, and you may well be, but it's hard for your potential clients to believe this when everyone is saying the same thing and pushing the same message. Therefore you need to point out your competitive point of difference another way, and there's only four ways to do this. Your four CPOD options are: *Position, Price, Product* and *Service*. No matter how good you are, some clients will choose the closest business based on *Position*, so there's nothing you can do about that – let them go, they may have been blowflies. Therefore that now leaves three options, *Price, Product* and *Service*. I've already expressed my opinion on discounting and trying to compete on *Price*, so that is also eliminated from the equation, leaving only *Product* and *Service*.

PEOPLE WILL PAY A PREMIUM

Research shows that people will pay more for a premium product and service if they are given the choice to do so. This is why prestige cars are still driven, women wear diamonds, Gucci has not vanished, "Limited edition" products sell quickly, and people still choose to purchase VIP tickets at music, sporting and business events.

In 2012, on the same family trip as when we visited Disneyland we had the opportunity to visit Universal Studios. The following ticketing options were available; Standard day entry ticket $84, a front of line ticket $169, or a VIP ticket $299. I hate waiting in line, so for the added service of going straight to the front of the queue I was prepared to pay the $169 ticket price. Going to the front of the line and walking past people who had been waiting for 45 minutes was worth every additional dollar paid.

Two years later, in 2014, I booked another holiday to Los Angeles with my brother and son, and because we were going to visit Universal Studios again, we decided to purchase the $299 VIP tickets. We chose VIP tickets for two reasons: 1) we could all afford it, and 2) we were given the choice. And once again it was worth every cent, and was so much better than the front of line ticket purchased in 2012, and I would pay it again in a heartbeat.

In my own business I always focused my efforts towards providing a quality product and a consistent service. I never tried to compete on price. I know my prices were more expensive than my competitors, but I didn't care because I knew I also offered a far better service, and – based on my business growth – my clientele agreed.

What is your CPOD going to be? If you give it some thought you'll be surprised what you can discover about your own business:

- Do you currently provide a service not offered by anyone else?

124

- Do you have a particular skill or expertise in a unique area of your industry? I have a friend, Craig McCahon, who is a Sign Writer, and when he learnt his trade he was taught how to do freehand sign writing, and this old-school skill gives him an edge over his competitors who only know how to use computers.

- Do you offer a guarantee on your product?

- Do you have an exclusive product?

- Do you provide a higher quality product?

- Does your product last longer than your competitors'?

- Can you make it more quickly?

- Is it made locally and not imported?

BRAND VS PRODUCT

Your CPOD is what makes your business different; it's what makes you stand out from the crowd and it helps strengthen your *brand positioning,* but to understand brand positioning you first need to understand the difference between a *brand* and a *product.* For example, in Australia:

- Panadol is a brand and paracetamol is the product.

- Panamax is a brand and paracetamol is the product.

Both brands contain the identical product and both do the same job, but the majority of people still choose Panadol over Panamax because of brand positioning and the perception of higher quality, even though Panamax is cheaper. It's crazy really, *but perception is everything.*

So how does this relate to you and your business? Well, your business name is your brand and what you do, and your occupation/trade is your product. You may agree or disagree, but everyone in your industry, in your area, has the same product, but what they don't have is your brand name, meaning your business name. This is why your business name holds so much value and why you need to protect it.

I recently saw the movie *Founder*, the true story of how Ray Kroc became the owner of the McDonald's Corporation. There was one particular scene in the movie that really captured my attention and drove home the power of branding. Ray Kroc, played by Michael Keaton, is talking to one of the McDonald brothers just after purchasing their business for two million dollars. He explained that their system of making burgers was great, but what he really wanted – more than anything else – was the name McDonald's. He could see the value is in the name, something even the two McDonald brothers could not see.

McDonald's, Disney, Nike, Apple and Microsoft are all brand names that wield so much power. A local accountant can probably do your tax return just as well as KPMG, but KPMG is now a massive brand, and they didn't achieve this by being the cheapest. You'll know when your brand is really strong because people will assume it's part of a bigger chain or franchise.

I know you may be thinking your business is completely different to the other businesses in your area, but your potential clients don't have a clue. They assume you were all trained the same way and you're not in jail, so it's only logical to think you're all the same, which is why you need to create a brand about your business name. Your brand positioning is the *"perception"* you create in the client's mind about your brand (your business) in relation to your competitor's brand (their business).

What *perception* are you trying to create about your brand?

- The *"most"* technical.

- The *"most"* efficient.

- The *"best"* business to see in a particular niche or sub-niche.

Or are you creating a *perception* that you're the *"cheapest"* business in town? The magic word here is *perception*, because what someone perceives to be true is their reality. If your clients believe that your business is the best at something then that will be the message they will share with their friends and family. They will position your brand first before anyone else. Having a strong USP and knowing your CPOD are all simple building blocks that are necessary if you want to take your brand to the number one position in your area. Where do you think your business ranks right now?

> "Positioning is not what you do to a product. Positioning
> is what you do to the mind of the prospect."
>
> Al Reis

It's no secret…there's money in small business, however you must understand the power of your brand and where it is positioned.

After reading this chapter, what ideas are going through your head? Write them down *right now*.

_____

_____

_____

_____

_____

_____

_____

SEVEN MYTHS SURROUNDING MARKETING

Many business owners feel that marketing is deceptive, which is a shame because if you want a successful business you're going to have to learn how to market yourself and your business. Marketing is merely the transfer of information from one person to another person, so if you hate the word *marketing*, replace it with *exchanging information*, because that's all you're really doing. Below are seven common myths that I believe are holding people back from marketing their businesses effectively.

MYTH 1: IF I DO MARKETING I'LL BE PROMOTING MY COMPETITORS

Yes you will; when you advertise, everybody benefits, so get over it and move on. If your competitors do get a piece of the pie, say 10%, from your marketing efforts and you're getting 90% of the pie, does it really matter? I would much rather eat 90% of a pie than have no pie at all. Even though your competitors get a small piece, what they won't get is to own *that space*. What do I mean by *that space?* If you get in first and tell a story and exchange information with your target market, you will own that message...you will own *that space*, and no one can ever take that away from you. Owning *that space* is extremely valuable and it also helps build your brand.

If another business tries to tell the same story, your target market will be aware that they are just trying to copy you and will think of your business first because you own *that space*. Think about this – which burger franchise does breakfast? You know the answer; it's McDonald's. They started advertising breakfasts first, and now they own *that breakfast space*. I know Hungry Jack's (Burger King), KFC and Subway have attempted to move into that breakfast space, but unfortunately it's already taken.

MYTH 2: MARKETING IS JUST ADVERTISING ISN'T IT?

No it isn't. Advertising is one small part of your overall marketing plan. It's like looking at the front of a building and saying you can see the whole building.

Placing an advertisement in the newspaper is advertising... it's the front of the building, but the "message" in your advertisement, the layout, the positioning, your text, the font, the newspaper you select and which day of the week you choose is marketing. Marketing is looking at the whole building in detail.

MYTH 3: MARKETING IS UNPROFESSIONAL

Yes it can be unprofessional, especially when it is done badly, but how can it be unprofessional to tell a client that you have the solution to their long-term problem? How is it unprofessional to let clients know you are open on weekends, especially if they live out of town and cannot come to you during the week?

As you can see, it's not the *exchange of information* that is unprofessional; it's how it is done. Offering a client an inducement is unprofessional, however I believe offering discounts to attract clients is no better.

MYTH 4: MARKETING IS EXPENSIVE

Marketing is only expensive if you don't get a return on your investment. Marketing is an investment, not an expense. To me marketing was always a long-term investment in my business and in my family's future. Marketing doesn't always have to cost you money; some marketing just requires you to invest your time.

MYTH 5: MARKETING ATTRACTS BAD CLIENTS

This is not true. Good marketing will never attract bad clients; however bad marketing will attract bad clients, especially if your message is too broad and not focused. If you aim your marketing message at your target market you have far more chance of attracting the type of client you want at your business, however if you do happen to get a few blowflies, don't be concerned; send them to your competition.

MYTH 6: MARKETING TAKES A LOT OF TIME

Marketing does not take a lot of time, but yes it does take some time and every business owner should be prepared to spend a few hours per week thinking about past, present and future marketing activities. A few hours per week can easily be done after hours, and you can do it with or without red wine.

It is extremely important to evaluate your marketing and to be able to gauge its effectiveness, but don't panic, you can have your team assist you. Many business owners think they have to do everything themselves, but you don't have to. By getting your team involved you also build team belief in what you are doing and they'll understand what you're trying to achieve. You should also set time aside for brainstorming sessions with your team, because you cannot come up with all the good ideas yourself.

MYTH 7: I'LL NEED TO PAY BIG DOLLARS TO GET A BUSINESS COACH

Once again, not true. Reading books, such as this awesome book you have in your hands right now, is the first step towards becoming your own expert. Reading books is almost like having a business coach right there with you, except you can't ask questions. If you really enjoy a book, make sure you read it a second or third time.

If the author has a website, as I do (tysonfranklin.com), visit it on a regular basis because new ideas are always being developed and posted. More than likely they will have a blog, and if they have a newsletter, sign up for it, because you can always unsubscribe. The other reason you should visit an author's website is that he or she cannot include every thought or idea in one book – it's impossible. So, a website is a great place to add information that didn't make the book or a place to add new thoughts and ideas. You should also listen to podcasts and watch YouTube and Facebook videos when you can, and follow inspiring people you come across. There is so much information online you could devour it 24/7, and I recommend you do this often, but not in the mornings; that's for creation, not consumption.

> **"Who you are in five years' time will be determined by the books you read and the people you associate with."**
>
> Charles Tremendous Jones

Coaching itself though is not overly expensive, especially if it gives you a great return on investment. If you do decide to get a business coach, get something in writing regarding the expected increase in revenue from using their services, but be prepared to do some work yourself because it won't all be done for you. A business coach is there to coach you, just like a football coach; they're not there to go out on the field and take the big hits for you. If a business coach says they can increase your business by 10%, tell them to go away because I think you'll get a 10% increase just by reading this book and visiting my website. If you only want a 10% increase, you don't need to do anything further than apply what you've learnt here. However, if you want more than 10% then you may need a business coach.

After reading this chapter, what ideas are going through your head? Write them down *right now*.

_____

_____

_____

_____

_____

_____

_____

_____

RUN, REST AND REPEAT YOUR MARKETING

Marketing that works today may not be effective tomorrow, and you need to know when your marketing message has become ineffective. One clear sign may be your telephone has stopped ringing, but this doesn't mean your marketing is no longer any good, it just means it may need to be put on the shelf for a while and reintroduced at a later date, especially if it has been proven to work well in the past.

I designed a newspaper advertisement in 1998 that is an absolute gem and up until selling my business I still used it, relatively unchanged, because it worked every single time I ran it. However, after a period of time it always becomes ineffective, and when this happened I'd give it a spell, just like a good racehorse. This one newspaper advertisement made my business in excess of a million dollars, if not more, which is why I refer to this advertisement as my *Black Caviar*. You just know whenever you run it, it's going to be a winner, but eventually it still needs to be rested because all advertising can become tired.

For those people who don't know, Black Caviar is a retired Australian thoroughbred racehorse that created history by being undefeated after 25 races.

BE CREATIVE AND THEN BE BORING

Having a good marketing plan is about being creative and then being boring. This may sound like a contradiction, but let me explain. Once you create a marketing idea that works and produces positive results consistently, you need to just keep repeating it. It may seem really boring, but boring is good, especially if it keeps producing positive results. When it stops being effective and begins to slow, put it on the shelf and give it a rest.

After a period of time, dust it off and use it again. If it produces amazing results again, you've found yourself a *Black Caviar*. I also developed a killer radio advertisement that I used for years, and my radio rep at the time kept asking me when I was going to change it because, as she put it, *"It's getting a little boring"*. My response: "I'll change it when it stops working."

TESTING AND MEASURING – MORE NUMBERS TO LOOK AT

So how do you develop a Black Caviar advertisement? Well, just like a good racehorse, it's something you develop over time, and the best way to do this is by testing and measuring. Testing and measuring is a technique used to determine the effectiveness of a marketing idea. In simple terms you test (or *try*) a new marketing idea and then measure the results. Testing and measuring is a process; it's not a destination. It's not an activity you do once and never do again. Just like a racehorse, you don't train it once and never train it again, instead it's something you constantly work on, tweak and improve upon.

For example, if you're thinking about dropping off 5000 flyers in one area with the same headline, a better idea would be to drop off five batches of 1000 flyers with five different headlines and see which headline produces the best result. If one particular flyer shines above the rest then you know you have a winner and this is the one you should use again.

Only test and measure one change at a time

With any marketing idea, only test and measure one change at a time. If you change the headline on your flyer, just make that one change and nothing else. Don't change the headline, the text, the layout and the distribution area, because there is no way of determining what change worked best. However, you can test and measure more than one marketing idea at one time. You could be testing and measuring a newspaper ad, a flyer and also an online Facebook ad because they are different marketing ideas.

> "Marketing without data is like driving
> with your eyes closed."
>
> Dan Zarrella

Never use phone activity to indicate the success or failure of a marketing campaign

The number of telephone calls you receive from a marketing campaign does not always equate to a successful campaign. This is also the power of testing and measuring. You may receive a lot of telephone calls from a particular advertisement, but unless those calls are converted to sales the campaign was not a success. You may receive fewer calls from a different campaign, but if every call is converted to a sale, resulting in repeat business and further referrals, then it was a successful campaign.

The type of clients you attract can also indicate if a campaign was a success or failure. If you wanted to attract a particular type of client, and you didn't, then the campaign was a failure. When you don't get the desired results from your campaign things must change.

Your goal with marketing is to eliminate losing campaigns and find winning campaigns. When you find winners, run them again and again, and if they continue to be winners, you may have found a Black Caviar.

It's no secret…there's money in small business, but you have to develop some Black Caviar marketing campaigns.

After reading this chapter, what ideas are going through your head? Write them down *right now*.

_____

_____

_____

_____

_____

_____

_____

BEWARE, THERE'S A SALES REP COMING TO SEE YOU

Have you ever considered swimming in a pool of sharks without a safety cage? Probably not, but this is exactly what you do when you begin to advertise. You will attract the attention of many Sales Representatives from various media outlets, all wanting to sign you up as a client. Now, I'm not saying all Sales Reps are sharks, however they will begin to circle like sharks when they become aware of fresh blood in the marketing waters. You need to realise that all Sales Reps pay close attention to their opposition media outlets, so if you begin your advertising campaign by placing an ad in the local newspaper, expect a call within weeks, if not days, from other local newspapers and magazines in your area. This will be followed by local radio and television Sales Reps, and so on. In addition to your traditional Sales Reps, you'll begin noticing a plethora of emails flooding your inbox from their online counterparts.

NEVER SIGN ANYTHING ON THE FIRST MEETING

If a Sales Rep says you need to sign today to get a particular deal, just walk away and tell them you need time to consider their proposal, because a good deal today should be a good deal tomorrow. I've rarely seen a marketing proposal that couldn't wait at least a week. At your first meeting you want to send a strong message to the Sales Rep that you're not an idiot or easy target and you're not going to sign the first thing they put in front of you. This is when advice from a business coach or experienced business friend can be invaluable.

Basically you need to give yourself time to weigh up the positives and negatives of any proposal and also look at the financial implications for your business. It's often said that you cannot polish a poo, but a crafty Sales Rep can get pretty close to making it sparkle, and their job is to sell advertising, so that's their prime objective – whether you can or cannot afford it is not their concern. More importantly though, you need time to formulate a list of questions so you are prepared for your second meeting with the Sales Rep. *Yes that's correct, you will have a second meeting, because you're now going to tell them what it is you want.*

If you sign an agreement too early you may have missed a perfect opportunity to negotiate for added extras, not mentioned in the first meeting. For example, if a Sales Rep wants you to advertise for four consecutive weeks in the local newspaper, insist on editorial space, or enquire about free ad placements in their online product. If they say this is not possible, tell them this would have been beneficial and sealed the deal, but now you're not sure if advertising in their newspaper is right for your business. *Believe me, you will get the extras most times.*

Every Sales Rep has room to negotiate, regardless of what they tell you. Every Sales Rep has a monthly budget they must meet, so sometimes there can be some good deals available, you just have to be prepared to ask. If they won't budge on price, you may be able to negotiate other benefits such as free tickets or an invite to a sporting or networking event. I often received tickets to movie premieres, lunch invitations, invites to corporate boxes at sporting events, corporate golf days and restaurant and travel vouchers.

Even though the benefits from advertising may be great and sometimes a lot of fun, the bottom line is you want to generate business. This must be kept at the forefront at all times and this is something that your Sales Reps should also be reminded of, because occasionally they will come to you with a proposal that is complete rubbish and has little benefit to your business. If this happens too often, it's time to change Sales Reps or move away completely from the advertising company because it's a sign they are starting to take you for granted and they are not listening. A good Sales Rep should understand your business, your target market or markets, and also what motivates and interests you.

I once had the same Sales Rep, who worked at a local radio station, for about seven years, and we would meet once a month to discuss my previous month's advertising and my future plans. Over this seven-year period we developed a trusting relationship and she never once tried to sell me rubbish. Unfortunately she moved away and was replaced by a complete, utter dud. He departed three months later, and was replaced by another person just as incompetent. Combined, these two Sales Reps, over a six-month period, never visited my business and basically never attempted to develop a relationship with me; all they cared about was themselves. Needless to say, when my advertising contract came up for renewal I completely ignored it. Actually… that's not exactly true: my incompetent Sales Rep forgot to present the new advertising proposal to me, and by the time she realised, I had moved on.

HAVE YOU ANY IDEA WHAT I DO?

When a Sales Rep meets with you for the first time, let them talk and then politely ask, *"So, do you know what I do?"* Wait quietly for their response. It's not a trick question, you're merely finding out their knowledge about your business, which is important if they have approached you with a specific advertising proposal that is supposedly perfect for you. If their perception of your business is wrong then the proposal they present to you will also be wrong.

Often they will tell you this type of broad advertising is called "branding" and it suits every business, but that's rubbish. Be honest and tell them you don't want branding, you want results.

DEMOGRAPHICS

Demographics are the quantifiable statistics of a given population, which when used in marketing can be very powerful, because this information helps reduce the costs of wasted marketing as it helps you become more targeted. If a Sales Rep tells you they have a particular product that is absolutely perfect for your demographic, you should ask them, *"So tell me, what is my demographic?"* You'll learn they often have no idea, but this is not surprising considering they often have no idea about your business, as we've already discussed.

So not only do you need to educate them about your business, you need to also educate them on who your "target market" is. This Sales Rep should leave and come back to you with a new proposal. Don't tolerate proposals that have not been properly thought through.

REACH VS FREQUENCY

Reach and frequency are terms often used by Sales Reps to assist in selling their marketing product. Basically *reach* is the number of people that will see your marketing message, whereas *frequency* is about how many times they will see it.

So here's the million-dollar question: is it better to make contact with 80 potential clients one time (*reach*), or is it better to make contact with only 20 potential clients four times (*frequency*)? A Sales Rep will tell you that they are both as important as each other, however they are completely wrong. I'll say that again – they are completely wrong because:

Reach without frequency = Wasted money

Marketing is about building a long-term relationship with your potential clients. This is why it is important for your marketing message to be consistent and repetitive, to the point of almost being boring. The more often you share your marketing message with a potential client – the frequency – the more chance you have of them responding.

One advertisement in a newspaper, with a large distribution, is a waste of money. Yes, I'm sure you will receive telephone calls on the publication day, especially if you have a really strong message and call to action, but you will receive a better response if you run a similar advertisement numerous times.

Think about this: have you read the newspaper today, or did you watch television yesterday? Did you read an article online this morning? If so, can you recall any advertisements? Only advertisements with *frequency* will be remembered, the others will be totally lost, unless of course they were unique and made you laugh, or you just happen to be the perfect target market and the message spoke directly to you.

To give you a good example of frequency; there's a business in the Atherton Tablelands called Golden Drop Winery, and they have been advertising on television for years. I think I could almost repeat their television commercial verbatim because I have seen it so many times, but here's the kicker: I don't think I have ever seen their television commercial on before 11 pm. Advertising on late night television is dirt cheap, and because it's so cheap they can repeat their television commercial over and over again, *and their ad has never changed.*

Now if they went for reach they could have advertised during *The X Factor*. The only problem would have been their budget; it would have been blown after one or two commercials. Reach is very expensive, whereas frequency is inexpensive, but you need to find the happy medium between the two. Of course if you have the budget of Coca-Cola you can smash reach and frequency, but small business owners don't have that size budget.

LISTEN TO THE FARMER

Here's a great analogy for you to consider: imagine a farmer with 500 fruit trees. The trees need to be fertilised twice each year for them to produce fruit, but the farmer only has enough fertiliser to fertilise them all just once. What should he do? Does he put fertiliser on all 500 trees once (reach), knowing it will produce zero fruit for the season, or should he only fertilise 250 trees twice (frequency), knowing it will produce fruit on 250 trees? Of course the farmer will choose option two as fruit from 250 trees is better than no fruit from 500 trees. Fruit puts money on the table and so will frequency.

So the next time you're considering doing a letterbox drop, instead of having ten thousand flyers delivered once (reach), consider only delivering two thousand flyers, but repeat it five times in the same area (frequency). This also gives you a chance to Test and Measure different headlines; therefore it's a double bonus.

If you have an online business and all your marketing is online, you can ignore flyers, television, radio, and so on, and change the terminology to suit what works best for you. Frequency and reach still works the same way on Facebook and other platforms. You can narrow or broaden your audience by age, location, occupation and many other parameters, and then you select your budget. Are you going to smash your whole budget in one day to 100,000 people (reach), or will you narrow your audience to 10,000 people, or less, and spread your budget out over one or two weeks, hitting the same people multiple times (frequency)?

WHO IS EDUCATING YOU?

As a general rule you should never get your marketing education from the same person who is trying to sell you advertising, and this applies to all forms of advertising, both offline and online. The Sales Rep has one job to do: sell you advertising. And that's exactly what they're going to do. It's not their fault if you're naïve.

I previously mentioned when I first moved to Cairns from the Gold Coast that my business boomed, even without me gaining any additional business knowledge. But in all the excitement, I almost went broke because I signed up for advertising that was truly a bad fit for my business and my target market. I was led to believe that *reach* was more important than *frequency*, and I overspent and blew my marketing budget. It was a very painful learning experience, and it took me a few years to fully recover, but there was no one to blame other than myself. Hindsight is a great teacher, and this is why I know for a fact you need to understand marketing, even if it's just the basics.

If your Sales Rep invites you to a marketing workshop put on by their company, it's okay to attend, just don't sign anything at the event and be aware that their opinions will be biased. Radio is always better than television – just ask your Radio Rep. And television is far better than radio – just ask your Television Rep. And newspaper advertising trumps them both – just ask your Newspaper Rep. And if you were confused about online marketing versus traditional offline marketing, don't be concerned because they will both tell you why their product is better, and they can even back it up with statistics and flashy charts, so they must be right.

MEDIA AND ADVERTISING AGENCIES

You may think it's easier to work with a media and advertising agency instead of individual Sales Reps and this may be true, because you only have to deal with one shark instead of a pack of sharks, but remember one big shark can do more damage and do it faster than a pack of smaller sharks just taking a small bite. The big difference with a media and advertising agency, though, is they will help you plan your media campaign as well as buying advertising space on your behalf, so if you're busy this may suit you perfectly, however you really need to check the credentials of the company before committing. Who have they worked with in the past? Can you contact any past clients? If the media agency is just a one-person company with a business name, you want to see their résumé and review their experience. Check them out just like you would any employee.

BEWARE THE CON

If you're approached with an advertising proposal over the telephone, always request information via email and ask for a contact number so you can call them back and verify their existence.

A few years back my Receptionist received a telephone call from a Police Officer wanting to urgently speak with the business owner. Well, of course they got me because it was the Police. When I got on the telephone he quickly explained it was not a Police matter, so there was no need to be concerned. Instead, he was calling to find out if I wanted to advertise in the local Police Journal.

I had come highly recommended, but he couldn't recall the person (*of course not because he was making it up*). After his long speech he informed me I could pay via credit card, over the telephone. I asked if he could email me the information so I could think about it and he said he couldn't because he didn't have an email account (*that's odd*). He also couldn't fax the information because he didn't have a fax machine, and finally he couldn't give me a return telephone number because he wasn't sure what the number was. When I asked which station he was located at, he hung up. *Yes*, it was a con, but I was very aware.

BUILDING RELATIONSHIPS

Don't get disheartened. Not all Sales Reps are trying to rip you off; some are honest people with a good product, and eventually you will develop close, trusting relationships with many of your Sales Reps as they get to know you and your business. In fact, over time they might become close friends, and the long-term development of these relationships is an integral part of your overall business success and future expansion, if that's what you want to do. Just be aware that if you're dealing with a Sales Rep and you feel they're not listening, respecting or understanding you and your business, you need to request someone new. Seriously, don't put up with their rubbish, because they're working for you, you're not working for them.

It's no secret…there's money in small business, but you need to be alert when talking to Sales Reps and Media Agencies.

After reading this chapter, what ideas are going through your head? Write them down *right now*.

_____

_____

_____

_____

_____

_____

_____

USING MARKETING
PILLARS TO CREATE
BUSINESS STABILITY

Creating a successful marketing strategy involves many factors, and the most crucial of all is making sure your business has as many referral sources as possible, meaning it has many ways of attracting new clients. It's dangerous to rely on just one or two predominant referral sources, because no matter how good they are, if one disappears, so does half or all your income. Instead, you should have dozens and dozens of referral sources, which when grouped together become what I call a *Marketing Pillar*. A pillar is basically a supporting structure that props up another object; in this particular case your Marketing Pillars are used to support and prop up your business.

In 438 BC in Ancient Greece, the Parthenon was built. If you ever see a picture of this amazing structure you'll notice the number of large pillars used to support its massive ceiling, and after 2500 years it is still standing and a recognisable structure today.

You need to look at your business in a similar way; *your business* is the ceiling and your referral sources – when grouped together – are the Marketing Pillars. There are six Marketing

Pillars that should be created for your business: Professional, Non-Professional, Internal, External, Verbal and Online.

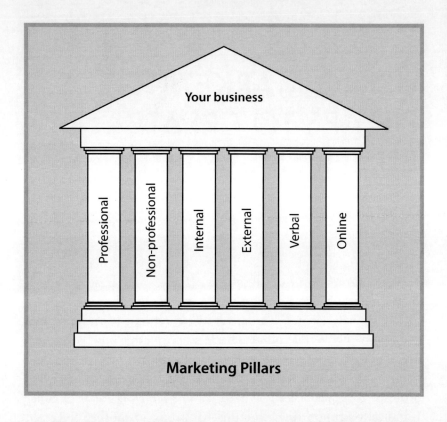

There are also no limits to the number of referral sources you can develop within each Marketing Pillar, and the more you develop, the further it strengthens and stabilises the Marketing Pillar. Also, the stronger the Marketing Pillars, the less chance you'll notice a financial downturn if one referral source, within a pillar, suddenly crumbles. You should constantly be nurturing and maintaining your referral sources and also be adding new referral sources to each Marketing Pillar, for further stability.

So how do you group your referral sources into Marketing Pillars? I don't think there is a right or wrong way to do this as long as it makes sense to you, and every industry is going to be different, however here is an example of how I grouped my referral sources together into Marketing Pillars:

- *Marketing Pillar One: professional referrers:* This comprises all marketing activities that involve direct referrals from people within your own industry. For example, in the health industry a Physiotherapist receiving a referral from a GP, an Accountant receiving a referral from a Lawyer, or a Carpenter receiving a referral from a Plumber. Professional referrers are industry specific.

- *Marketing Pillar Two: non-professional referrers:* This group comprises referrals from businesses outside your industry. A Lawyer or Carpenter could receive a referral from the local Hairdresser.

- *Marketing Pillar Three: internal marketing:* This involves everything you do within your business that the general public does not see until they step inside your business to make an enquiry or become a client.

- *Marketing Pillar Four: external marketing:* This involves all your visual and auditory advertising directed towards people in your target markets who are not yet clients.

- *Marketing Pillar Five: verbal marketing:* This involves all communications you have with the broader market by way of public speaking, networking events, business lunches, trade shows and the like.

- *Marketing Pillar Six: online marketing:* This involves every activity your business does online, including your website, blogs, social media pages, audio accounts, video channels, and apps.

Your Marketing Pillars are the most crucial and important aspect of your business, and because of this I'm going to dedicate a complete chapter to each one, so it can be discussed in more detail.

Some chapters will be longer than others, but don't discount their value based on size. Also, you'll notice some marketing activities can live in more than one Marketing Pillar.

"You can't sell anything if you can't tell anything."

Beth Comstock

After reading this chapter, what ideas are going through your head? Write them down *right now*.

_____

_____

_____

_____

_____

_____

_____

MARKETING PILLAR ONE: PROFESSIONAL REFERRERS

There is a strong correlation between the number of referrals your business receives and your ability to stay connected with your professional referrers. Your goal is to stay top of mind, because you want to be thought of first, not last, when they're choosing someone from your industry. The more often you're seen and heard, the more often referrals will flow your way, so be very visible and loud. Your professional referrers also see the same marketing messages your clients see, so consider your message carefully. Does your message say you're the cheapest, fastest, or most advanced? Once you start receiving referrals, remember to maintain the relationship because client referrals you receive today could be gone tomorrow, and it can happen fast.

CREATING AND MAINTAINING RELATIONSHIPS

Some professional referrers will begin referring to you immediately and then suddenly stop referring. This can happen for many reasons, but the most obvious reason is they've started referring back to the person they've used for years. It's nothing against you personally, but a one-off meeting you had six months ago is not going to cement your relationship nor will it break a referral habit. To break this habit, a new habit must be created, which is why you need to stay in regular contact.

But what does it mean if you've been receiving referrals for years and then suddenly they stop? It could mean they're referring their clients to a new person who made a personal visit to see them; however there can be other reasons. For example, if you're an Accountant receiving referrals from a Lawyer and the Lawyer's brother opens an accounting business, it's almost guaranteed you will lose these referrals.

When I had my business on the Gold Coast there was another business that referred a lot of people to me, then suddenly the referrals stopped. I was a little concerned, so I went and saw them and asked if there was a problem, and their reason was very simple. They told me there was a new business in town and the owner of the business had big boobs. I gave this answer some thought and concluded I wasn't prepared to get a boob job, so I lost his referrals. The point I'm trying to make is sometimes it's out of your control, but at other times it may well be your fault.

Ask yourself, when was the last time you made contact with your professional referrers? Do you even know who your potential professional referrers are? If you're in the health industry, everyone else in the health industry is a potential professional referrer. If you're in the finance or business industry, it works the same way. In the building industry you have other trades that could directly refer clients to you. There are no exceptions.

If you can't remember the last time you made contact with your professional referrers, it was too long ago. Here are some ideas you can start using immediately to reconnect and stay connected.

Personal visits

Nothing beats a one-on-one meeting, because it gives you both a chance to put a face to a name. This is also a great time to leave business cards and other information about your business.

If you're leaving business cards and brochures, make sure you provide your own holders, especially if you're expecting them to leave them on a counter top or display; otherwise they will be thrown out. Also make it a habit to return regularly because if a brochure holder becomes empty it will be removed or used by someone else. *This is why I had my own brochure holders embossed with my business name, so they cannot be used by another business.*

Rate the visit

After your first visit, give it a rating out of 10 and write notes about how you felt the meeting went. What went well, and is there anything you could do better next time? These notes are gold, and are valuable for your future meetings. If during your meeting you noticed a picture on the wall of them at a whisky distillery in Scotland, keep a note. If they mention a family holiday, ask about their family. How long have they been married, and how many kids do they have? Developing long-term relationships is all about communication, and the more questions you can ask the more you will learn.

All this information needs to be documented and saved. Here's an interesting point though; don't be surprised if some of your meetings that you rate 10 out of 10 give you no referrals, whereas some of your 2 out of 10 meetings give you many referrals. Sometimes there's no logic.

Say thank you

When a client is referred, always acknowledge the referral and say thank you to the referrer. You may send a simple email, a thank you card, or you may drop off a bottle of nice wine or bottle of spirits (*remember the whisky distillery photo*), depending on how valuable the referral was. I've referred a lot of people over the years to various businesses, and I know some of them have made thousands of dollars off my referrals and I didn't even get a thank you. Well, not until I brought it up when I saw them next – *"Oh yeah, thanks for that referral Tyson"*. Do you think I referred many more after that? People don't necessarily want their butts smooched, but they do want to be acknowledged and thanked.

Simple emails

Over time you need to gather as many email addresses as possible and add them to your database. Using an email database is an inexpensive way of staying in regular contact with your professional referrers, and it should be updated annually. When it comes to sending emails, just make sure you have a valid reason for contacting them, otherwise you will become annoying. Keep emails simple and stick to the facts, with information such as:

- change in trading hours
- new equipment
- new services
- new team members.

Email newsletters

Email newsletters can contain more information than a simple email, however they must still be informative, otherwise a professional referrer won't want to read them. Email newsletters are inexpensive and a great way to – for example – promote an upcoming event, and also an opportune time to discuss seasonal activities, but don't make the newsletter all about your business or industry, otherwise it can be boring. I'm sure my Accountant, Lawyer and even my Swimming Pool Maintenance guy could create an informative newsletter that I'd find interesting to read, however it can't be all about accounting, law or pool maintenance. Add in jokes, recipes, wine and whisky reviews. Find out what your readers are interested in and entertain them. At the same time you can add an article about your business, what you do, or a special promotion. *Subscribe to my newsletter at www.tysonfranklin. com and you'll see what I mean.*

Once you start a monthly or weekly email newsletter campaign you must maintain it and make sure it is sent about the same time each month or week.

Even though email newsletters are inexpensive and work well, they can also have limitations if there are many professional referrers working at the same premises and they share a common email address. If this is the case, you should try to obtain individual or personal email addresses wherever possible.

Alternatively, it may be worth sending a hard-copy newsletter as well, personally addressed to each professional referrer. Hard-copy newsletters are statistically far more effective than email newsletters, however hardly anyone does them anymore because they're more expensive and time consuming to produce, but if you do one it will be noticed. When was the last time you received a hard-copy newsletter from a business? And when it arrived, did you read it? You probably did because you don't receive many hard-copy newsletters. And how many email newsletters do you receive each month, and how many do you open and read? You probably don't open too many at all. So consider going old school with newsletters and see what happens.

The Golden Goose

Are you aware that in most businesses the Office Manager makes most of the daily decisions, because that's what they are employed to do? They are the person who decides what brochures will be displayed in the front office, who is on their referral speed dial, and who can and cannot get a meeting with the business owners. This is why you need to try to build a relationship with the Office Managers, because they are the Golden Goose.

Taking one Office Manager to an informal lunch is a great way to build a lasting relationship, but here is an idea worth considering: organise an Office Managers' Lunch. *Every town has a local business club or organisation that meets on a monthly basis, and they usually have an interesting guest speaker, so these lunches are perfect. Depending on your budget you may only book a few seats to begin with, but ideally you want to book a table of 10, and make sure you take your own Office Manager if you have one. Getting Office Managers on your side is almost like insider trading, but a more legal version. Plus, Office Managers talk to other Office Managers, so they're great at increasing your word-of-mouth advertising. Booking a table of 10 may cost you $450 to $750, but compare this to other forms of advertising and you'll find it's great value.*

Professional referrers survey

Each year you should send a well-thought-out survey to all your professional referrers. I say 'well thought out' because the information you gather from a survey is only as good as the questions you ask. Poor questions = Poor answers, which results in a pointless survey. The purpose of your survey is to gather valuable feedback about how you are being perceived by your professional referrers and the clients they're referring. Your clients may never tell you directly they have a problem, but they will share it with the person who referred them. Don't expect positive comments from everyone, and in fact you want a few negative comments because they give you an opportunity to improve your service.

Do not email this survey; it's best to mail or hand deliver it instead, and make sure you enclose a reply paid envelope for its return, or you can schedule a time to return and pick it up. Once again, producing a hard-copy survey will cost more and be more time consuming, however it will be far more effective than an emailed version. Information from surveys is important and you want as many back as possible, so "go hard".

Acknowledge a significant day

Professional referrers receive numerous cards and gifts at Christmas time, none of which are probably remembered, therefore choose a different day to say "thank you". Pick any other significant day of the year and celebrate it in style. In Australia it could be Australia Day, or in the United States it could be Independence Day. The day you choose is not relevant, it's about standing out from the crowd because nobody else will do it.

Acknowledging a significant day can be achieved by sending a simple card, or you can invest a little more money and organise bottles of wine through a corporate wine supplier, with personalised labels. I have done this on many occasions; it is an absolute winner and a great way to stay in touch. *Warning: make sure you taste the wine because you don't want to send rubbish wine.* I used to also attach a light-hearted cover letter explaining my commitment, and letting them know I had to visit the Barossa Valley especially and taste over 20 wines just to make sure I chose the right wine for them…because I cared.

Third-party events

A third-party event is where you piggyback off another organisation's event and use it to promote your business to your clients. A great example of a third-party event is a charity golf day. It's a simple concept: you enter a team, pay the team fees and invite people you would like to spend four to five hours with. Entering a team can cost as little as $450.

Corporate boxes at sporting events work in a similar fashion. I organised a corporate box at a rugby match and it cost me $1500 for the day including food and alcohol, and I was able to invite 10 people. I received over $3000 in referral business the following week, and I continued to receive referrals for many years afterwards, so it was a great investment.

Information evenings

If you introduce a new service or facility or unique piece of equipment to your business you should inform all your professional referrers, and the best way to do this is to organise an information evening. Information evenings can be a lot of fun, and it's a great opportunity to also show off any new team members. Of course not everyone is going to attend an information evening, which is expected, but by at least sending out an invitation you have not only informed them about your new product or service you have also kept the relationship connected.

But here's another thought: you don't have to have a new product or service to hold an information evening.

As I was writing this chapter I was invited to the FNQ Plastics (Cairns) quarterly information evening, by owners Colin and Lesley Van Staveren, and the purpose of the evening was to connect with local business people and to invite them into their business to check out their showroom and factory, so we could see what FNQ Plastics manufactured. Prior to this I had driven past their business hundreds of times, but never stopped, probably because I didn't need any plastic...or so I thought. They catered the event and also provided beer and wine, and throughout the evening they conducted tours of the factory. As I said, I didn't need plastic, but after seeing what they make and sell my mind has changed: I think I do need plastic in my life! This is a very simple yet brilliant idea, and I'm surprised more businesses don't do the same: invite other business people for an information evening to simply show off what they do. The night may have *cost them $1000, but I'm sure they will get a huge return on their investment. Basically they created a networking event in their own building, and as a side benefit, photos from the evening were posted on social media – and little did they know I would be mentioning their business in my book.*

Can you do something similar? Remember it's all about connecting and staying connected to your professional referrers.

Scan the local newspaper

You should make a habit of scanning the local newspaper to see if any new businesses have recently moved to the area, and if they have you should contact them before anyone else does. You could send them information about your business, but a better idea would be to drop off a $20 bottle of sparkling wine with a small card saying, *"Congratulations. Would love to catch up in the next few weeks for a coffee and see how we can be of benefit to each other".* Nothing beats a one-on-one meeting, and you should try to organise this as soon as possible.

If you think newspapers are dead and buried, think again. It's true they are struggling, but a lot of traditional businesses still advertise in the local paper when they first open, and if they've been smart with their PR they may also have provided the newspaper with a well-written media release, and this is exactly what you're looking for.

Opening party

If you're opening a new business or location, make sure you have an opening party. Don't let this opportunity slip past. You should invite every professional referrer you have met personally, or want to meet, and close friends and family, and really enjoy the night. Also invite the business editor of the local newspaper, editors from local magazines, and invite the managers from the local radio and television stations. Once again this is a perfect opportunity to share this event on social media.

Ongoing celebrations

Don't limit your celebrations to just your opening, or information evenings. If you renovate, expand or relocate, this is a good enough reason to celebrate. You can also celebrate milestones in business. Once again only your imagination limits you, and the costs to put on a decent party will depend on the numbers and quality of your catering.

Over a period of time you will begin to notice patterns starting to form with the amount of contact you have with a professional referrer versus the number of referrals you receive from them. It starts to become predictable.

It's no secret...there's money in small business, but you must make an effort to stay connected with your professional referrers.

After reading this chapter, what ideas are going through your head? Write them down *right now*.

_____

_____

_____

_____

_____

_____

MARKETING PILLAR TWO: NON-PROFESSIONAL REFERRERS

I define a non-professional referrer as any business or individual that has the ability to refer a client to your business, but they are outside of your specific industry. This Marketing Pillar is often neglected and unloved, but they can be one of your biggest sources of referrals. Because every industry is different, so are the types of non-professional referrers for each industry, but I'll share a few simple examples and let your imagination come up with the rest for your specific industry.

As I mentioned before, a Carpenter may have a professional referral relationship with a Plumber, an Electrician and other people in the building industry. A non-professional referrer could be the local hardware store, paint store, nursery or real estate office. Can you see how they relate and can refer clients? An Accountant may have a direct professional referral relationship with a Lawyer, Financial Planner and Finance Brokers, but have they considered their relationship with the staff at their local bank branches? There would be a lot of them.

However, don't limit yourself to the most obvious businesses; think outside the square. Where do you visit on a regular basis? What about:

- coffee shops – do you buy a coffee at a regular coffee shop?

- hairdressers – everyone gets their hair cut somewhere

- beauty salons – if it's not you, does you partner visit this type of business?

Once again you're only limited by your imagination.

TREAT THEM EQUALLY

You should treat your non-professional referrers with the same respect as you would your professional referrers – they deserve nothing less and they must be nurtured in a similar fashion. You should:

- add their details to your email database

- know the names of the business managers

- send cards and bottles of wine if they're referring clients

- invite them to third-party events

- invite them to lunches

- invite them to information evenings and parties.

If you have to ask yourself if someone should or should not be added to your list of non-professional referrers, then the answer is they should, because they can always be removed later if the relationship is not working.

Once you have their details in your database you need to maintain regular contact with them. Don't try to shove your business down their throat or leave business cards and flyers on their counter top, even if you think they need your services or their clients would benefit by knowing what you have to offer. If you build a good relationship with them, they may eventually ask you for business cards or flyers before you get a chance to offer.

> "Referrals aren't given easily. If you don't take the time to establish credibility, you're not going to get the referral. People have to get to know you. They have to feel comfortable with who you are and what you do."
>
> Ivan Misner

COFFEE IDEAS

Here's two ideas every business can do, regardless of their industry. They won't cost you a lot to implement, they would be easy to test and measure for success, and they will cement your relationship with your local coffee shop.

Here's the first idea: talk to the owner or manager and ask if you can sponsor the first 10 cups of coffee sold on a Monday morning. At $5 a cup it's only going to cost your business $50, and all you ask in return is when the coffee is handed over they say, *"This coffee has been paid for by company ABC"*. If the coffee shop also agreed to hand out your business card with each cup of coffee that would be great, or even better and if you had the time and you were having a coffee yourself on Monday morning, they could say, *"This coffee has been paid for by company ABC, and the owner of the business is actually sitting over there"*. Now this may seem like a real shotgun approach because you don't exactly know who's buying the coffee, but it's not as broad as you think and you can narrow the market if you wish. You may stipulate it's for the first 10 men, women, people with children, men wearing suits, or whoever you want to target.

The second idea is much easier, and it's really just a thank you to your existing clients. Organise an account at a coffee shop in your local area and tell your clients all they need to do is hand over your business card for a free cup of coffee. Once again this will build your referral relationship with the coffee shop, and you should be able to arrange a discount for each cup of coffee.

With both your professional and non-professional referrers you should be aware that they may already work with another business in your area, but don't be shy – ask them up front which business they currently refer to and why. It could be they've never had a choice before because there was only one relevant type of business in the area...but now that they do have a choice you could be the one. On the other hand, their business of choice may be their brother, in which case you stand no chance, but knowing this information up front will save you a lot of time and money.

If they say they don't work with anyone, and if it suits your business and personality, immediately offer in-house training for their staff in whatever your area of expertise is. Let them know the better educated their team are, the more widgets or services they may sell (plus you'll get more referrals). If they say no to this offer then they probably work with someone already but didn't want to admit it.

If you're providing in-house training with their team you should be getting regular referrals. If this is not happening after a few weeks, you need to put your efforts elsewhere. Don't let anyone take advantage of you and your expertise. You need to make sure the relationship you're trying to build is reciprocal and not all one-way traffic, which can be the case with some businesses. They will take, take, take, and give nothing in return.

It's no secret...there's money in small business, however there needs to be a return on your efforts.

After reading this chapter, what ideas are going through your head? Write them down *right now.*

_____

_____

_____

_____

_____

_____

_____

_____

MARKETING PILLAR THREE: INTERNAL MARKETING

Internal marketing is all about marketing to your existing client database, and the best thing about this is you've already done all the hard work. You've already collected their details, because they've made a past enquiry and supplied you with their email or postal address, or they have used your services or purchased your product from you and are now a happy client.

YOUR CLIENT DATABASE IS GOLD

A lot of businesses undervalue their client database, not realising it is absolute gold, as is your professional and non-professional database. It's the one thing your competitors would love to get their hands on if they could.

As a business owner you should constantly be trying to add names and grow this database list. Your whole internal marketing strategy revolves around your client database, so never delete or archive a name unless the client asks to be removed, dies, or they move away.

I still kick myself today for deleting over 15,000 names from my original database, between 1992 and 2006, because I didn't understand the power and value of developing a good database. As you read through this chapter you'll understand why I should never have deleted these clients, but we all learn from our mistakes – and I confess I have made plenty of them.

Internal marketing is about business development and commitment to improving your clients' experience, which leads to long-term business success. You should constantly be promoting your services and products, and internal marketing is how you do it. If you choose not to educate your clients, don't be surprised when they go to another business for a service you actually offer.

Never assume they know about all the services you provide. If you want to test this theory, ask the next 10 clients you see to list the top five services your business offers. You may be surprised with the answers. I mentioned before that I've had my current accountant for over 10 years, but I've only been using his bookkeeper for the past one or two years because I didn't know his business offered this service, or if I did know I forgot. FNQ Plastics, the business I mentioned earlier, sells an extensive range of beer coolers, small, large and mega-sized, which I was unaware of until their information evening. Now I'm not sure if they produce a newsletter, but I do know they have an active Facebook page, so I hope they're telling people about this product, otherwise people will buy them from their competitors, and the problem when someone goes to your competitor is they may stay there.

Both these stories demonstrate why we need to always be educating our clients and why we should never assume they know what we do. Internal marketing is one of the cheapest forms of marketing, and sometimes it's the most cost effective and easiest to measure in results. Here are some internal marketing ideas you should consider if you're not already doing so. *They are definitely not in order of importance, and this is not a complete list of ideas – it's endless.*

TELEVISIONS

If you have a waiting area you should have a television promoting all the services you offer. You could have a DVD created by an audio-visual professional, or you could create something really simple yourself. There are many apps and inexpensive programs available that can assist you with this process. Recording and editing on your iPhone is fine, as long as you can get the lighting and sound right, but if you're going to produce a lot of visual promotions you may want to invest in better equipment.

If you have the space for a television screen, get one.

I'm not a huge fan of showing free-to-air television in a waiting area, for two reasons:

- the noise can be quite distracting
- there's the potential for a competitor's ad to be shown and that's not what you want.

However, when there is a special event on, such as the Australian Open tennis, the Olympics, the Super Bowl or even the Academy Awards, you probably should have it on, but at all other times use it to promote your business and the services and products it has to offer.

PUT UP SIGNS THAT SAY "WE HAVE A WEBSITE"

In your waiting area and in every room where a client may go you should have a sign, in full colour, mentioning your website and the social media sites your business is involved with.

Please Like, Follow and Review us on:

If nothing else, it will create conversation and drive more people to these online areas. Tell your clients the benefits of *liking* your social media pages, and if they're not sure what to do, give them instructions. Even better, hand them an instruction sheet on exactly how to do it because each social media site has a slightly different process to follow. You should become familiar with each site yourself.

PICTURES AND POSTERS ON YOUR WALLS

If it's not relevant to you, your family or your business, take it down. Ideally posters on the wall should be promoting other services you offer, or reflect something about you, and never put anything on the wall unless it's framed. If you're using sticky tape or Blu-Tack you should slap yourself. Picture frames where posters can be snapped in and out are perfect for internal marketing, because you can change the posters on a regular basis, and having one-off posters printed is quite inexpensive. If you store them correctly they will last for years.

Information posters should not be limited to your foyer or waiting area; you can have them in different rooms, on backs of doors and also in the bathroom. You could be quite humorous with your bathroom poster if you wanted to – *"now that you're seated and we have your full attention…* ". You'll find your A and B type clients appreciate good, light-hearted humour.

COMPANY AND BUSINESS BROCHURES

Brochures are an easy way to put all the services you provide into one simple document, and you should hand one to every client who enters your business. You do not need to do a massive print run initially, instead use the services of a graphic artist to help you get the design right, then go to the printers and have it professionally printed, in colour. You don't need thousands to get you started; just a short run of 150 or 200. Or, you can print them yourself if you have a good-quality laser printer. Never photocopy a brochure if you're running low, as a poor-quality copy will reflect poorly on your business.

All brochures should be placed in brochure stands and they should be easy to access. If you have the space, write a brochure for each of the services you provide, in addition to your overall business brochure.

CLIENT RECEIPTS

If you give your clients a receipt, why not print your receipts onto pre-printed flyers promoting another service that your business has to offer? The flyer can be black and white, but colour is far better. You could have more than one flyer and vary it based on the type of client receiving the receipt. For example, a client receiving a receipt from a lawyer for a property settlement could be sent a receipt and on the back they could be promoting the top five benefits of updating their will. A hairdresser could easily promote a new product in their salon or a new team member. What can you promote?

INTERNAL MARKETING SURVEYS

Every business wants more A and B clients, but how do you find them? One of the best ways is to create an internal marketing survey and ask your A and B clients some simple questions. For example:

- What radio station do you listen to?
    - local radio stations
    - national radio stations
    - I don't listen to the radio
- What times do you listen to the radio?
    - mornings
    - during the day
    - drive time
    - evenings
- What do you watch on TV?
    - Which TV stations?
        - free to air TV
        - pay TV
        - Netflix, etc.
    - What are your favourite programs?
- What do you read?
    - newspapers:
        - local
        - national
        - free weekly
- Do you read locally published magazines?

- How do you search for a business?
  - online search (Google, Bing, Yahoo, Yellow Pages Online, etc.)?
  - phone directory.

This information is extremely important when it comes to planning your future marketing, as you want to maximise your results by only attracting your target market, which is more A and B clients and fewer C and D clients. The results from your surveys will sometimes be the exact opposite to what your Sales Rep may be telling you about their marketing product.

I had a Sales Rep from a locally published free magazine visit me and they explained how good their publication was and why it would be perfect for my business. Fortunately, I had already started my internal marketing survey and found that none of my A and B clients liked this free magazine; however, clients that were identified as being C and D clients did read it and looked forward to it each month because it was free. Isn't that interesting?

ON-HOLD MESSAGES – YOU NEED THEM

When a client is placed on hold it can seem like an eternity, and if you're forcing them to listen to Richard Clayderman against their will it can seem even longer and is just plain mean – *unless of course you own a piano shop*. As an alternative, you could have the local radio station playing, but what if your competitor is advertising on the radio station at exactly the same time? You could lose that client. As an alternative, you should consider having an on-hold messaging system. Actually, you shouldn't just consider it… you should have it.

On-hold messages give your business a very professional, corporate image, which cannot be underestimated. Even as a sole operator you can create an image of being much larger than you really are. Remember: *perception is reality.* On-hold messages give your business a perfect opportunity to market to both new and existing clients.

If a client or potential client has to be put on hold for 60 seconds, why not tell them about your business in more detail? Tell them about the vast range of services you offer and the new services you've recently introduced. I've had many clients ask for more information about one of the messages they've heard while being on hold.

Another benefit of on-hold messages is your messages can be updated and changed throughout the year quite easily, usually at no extra charge. This is important because your business is constantly evolving, so you want your messages to evolve with your business.

ANSWERING MACHINE MESSAGES

Answering machine messages should always be short and to the point, and once again you have a captured audience so it's a perfect opportunity to leave a good first impression. Below are two answering machine messages. You determine which one sounds better:

- *Example one:* "Hello, you've called Company ABC. Our phone is currently unattended so please leave your name and telephone number after the beep and we will return your call as soon as possible. Thank you."

- *Example two:* "Hello and welcome to Company ABC. We're unable to answer the telephone right now, but would love the opportunity to return your call to discuss how we can be of service to you. After the beep, please leave your name and telephone number and one of our friendly team will get back to you as soon as possible. Once again, thank you for calling Company ABC, and we will be in touch with you shortly."

Can you see the difference between the two messages? There's nothing wrong with the first message, however the second message is by far more professional and shows a more appreciative attitude towards receiving the telephone call, because you *do* appreciate their telephone call – it's not a burden or interruption.

If you're planning to be closed for an extended period of time, outside of the normal public holidays, make sure you adjust your answering machine message with accurate and up-to-date information about your closure period. This is especially important over the Christmas holiday period because some businesses will close only for the public holidays while others will close for the full break over Christmas and New Year. Make sure you inform your clients when you will re-open. (I feel sorry for businesses that forget to update their answering machine message after the Christmas holidays, especially when it's March. Never a good sign.)

SIMPLE LETTERS

Sending a simple letter is still one of the easiest ways to stay in touch with your clients, yet it is often overlooked. A simple *thank you letter* will go a long way. Think about it… when was the last time you were thanked by a business for using their services? I've stayed in a lot of hotels and not once have I been thanked, even though I drop $200 to $300 per night, so does this make me want to stay there next time, or try somewhere else? However, they will send me an email asking me to review them on Trip Advisor, which I always do. Some places do get back to me after my review, which I do appreciate.

Look at every letter as an opportunity to promote your business further. Your thank you letter shows that you appreciate their business, and it is a perfect opportunity to enclose information about another service you may offer. The idea is to think...what do you do that this client may not know about? Then supply this information.

I've used approximately 20 different standard letters for various reasons. Some were recall letters, others were reactivation letters, and then I had standard letters designed to promote specific services and special offers throughout the year. These letters constantly evolved as my business evolved, and my client database determined what letters were sent and to whom. The bigger the client database, the more letters you can send, meaning the more response you will receive...meaning the more $$$$ you will make. This is why you shouldn't delete names from your database!

NEWSLETTERS

Whole books have been written about newsletters, so I'll keep this brief and straight to the point. Unless the newsletter has relevance to the client, it is a waste of time. If you prepare a newsletter, make sure it is all about the client and not you. Give them a reason to want to keep reading it. Make it valid and worthwhile. What's in it for them? This applies to both emailed and mailed newsletters.

EMAIL DATABASE

Using emails to stay in touch with clients is very inexpensive, fast, and an immediate way to communicate with clients about sudden changes within the business. Emailing is far more cost effective than sending mail, however *it's a proven fact that a letter addressed to a client is far more effective than an email.* How many emails do you receive and delete without opening? Probably a lot, and many you should have already *unsubscribed*. But how many personally addressed envelopes with a stamp do you throw out without opening? I would guess none. So, old-style mail is going to be far more effective than email, but it's slower and more expensive. However, if more clients open it, and it produces more sales, is it really more expensive?...*I think not.*

Using email to market to your clients is only effective if it's done properly. If you send too many pointless emails you will be added to the client's "junk" mailbox, and so you should be. The same rules apply when sending emails to clients as they do when sending emails to professional referrers. You need valid reasons to contact them, such as:

- a change in business hours

- closing and opening times over holiday periods

- a new service

- a "special offer".

SHORT MESSAGE SERVICE – 'SMS' (TEXT)

Sending short messages has become quite popular over the last few years, and many big companies have adopted this mode of communication. Just like emails, they are relatively inexpensive, fast, and can be sent to a large number of people at once. But with every piece of technology there will be advantages and disadvantages.

One of the big advantages of text messages is it's a very personal mode of communication because the message goes directly to the person you're trying to contact, and because we're all so used to communicating with friends and family this way it doesn't seem obtrusive when it arrives. Spam programs do not block text messages, as can happen to emails. However if your business repeatedly sends out the same message it can be annoying and reflect negatively on your business and the brand reputation you're trying to build. Text messages are quite short, so you need to learn how to be creative with your sentences. Sometimes it's far better to use fewer characters and say less than trying to say too much and making no sense.

Combining text messages with emails can also work very well, especially if you use the text as a teaser followed by the email that can contain far more information, links, photos and so on.

One big problem with technology is it's given us the ability to communicate badly with our clients, more often, so make sure you use it wisely.

CLIENT SATISFACTION SURVEYS

Client surveys are an excellent way to stay in touch with clients and also gain valuable information and feedback about your business and your team. Negative feedback should be viewed as an opportunity to improve. One negative comment means nothing, but if the same comment is being repeated then you need to address it.

With any survey, it's important to work out:

- What questions do you want to ask? Your questions will affect the answers.

- Which clients are you going to send it to?

- When will you send it? This can mean time of the year and also how long the client has been with your business.

You can have more than one survey, and surveys can be sent with other client letters. *You could send a survey with every new client thank you letter.* Always allow an area on your survey sheet for further comments from the clients, and make sure you have *reply paid envelopes* enclosed with your surveys to ensure you get more returns.

REVIEWING AND REACTIVATING CLIENT FILES

Even with the best systems in place, some clients still manage to fall through the cracks; therefore you should review all client files on a regular basis. This task is so important you should do it yourself until you have trained another team member to do this for you, but do not delegate this task too early. You need to thoroughly develop your system for reviewing past client files.

Your goal when reviewing client files is to look for irregularities and gaps. Of course every industry will have their own irregularities, but take a look at the examples below and see if they relate to your business:

- A client may have used your business every few months for the past five years and then suddenly stopped. Why hasn't your team pointed this out to you?

- You look at another client file and notice the last thing written was for the client to speak to their bank manager and then they were going to call you, but they never did. Once again, why? How did they fall through the cracks?

- After submitting a quote you're told they want to get started, but first they need to check with their business partner, but they never came back to you. Why?

The reason you look for irregularities is so you can fix them. You cannot fix something if you don't know it's broken. As soon as a possible irregularity has occurred you need to send the client a well-constructed letter to find out why they have not returned, or why they have stopped using your business. You could telephone the client, but a letter also gives you an opportunity to promote a new or existing service. This letter should be followed up with a phone call one week later. The more effort you put in now to retain your existing clients, the less money you will need to invest in the future to attract new clients. Client retention and reactivation is just as important, if not more important, than finding new clients.

KEEP INTERNAL MARKETING CONSISTENT

The most important part of internal marketing is consistency. Posters on walls, brochures, receipts and all correspondence should be consistent in *design, colours and fonts*, so it resonates familiarity about your business and over the long term forms part of your overall branding.

You should have a meeting with all team members *today* and discuss further ways to implement internal marketing.

It's no secret...there's money in small business, but you must show your existing clients you care, by staying in touch.

After reading this chapter, what ideas are going through your head?
Write them down *right now.*

_____

_____

_____

_____

_____

_____

_____

MARKETING PILLAR FOUR: EXTERNAL MARKETING

Internal marketing focuses solely on developing your existing clients' experience and knowledge about your business, whereas *external* marketing encompasses everything you do to attract new clients to your business. You're a business owner, therefore you need to be promoting your business from the time you leave your house until the time you arrive back home again; you need to be conscious of the fact that you're in marketing mode. This chapter is going to touch on some of the major areas of external marketing, however this list is far from complete.

START HERE: WORK SHIRTS

Before you do anything else, you need to have a work shirt with your logo proudly displayed. Yes, a work shirt is external marketing, and here's a simple truth: every successful business has one, and every unsuccessful or poorly run business does not. Isn't that interesting? It's important that every team member has a work shirt, and it should be worn every day. There are no excuses for it not to be worn. If you have a day off during the week you can still wear your work shirt, because it promotes your business.

When you are consistently marketing your business, your business name becomes very familiar; therefore a work shirt worn outside of the business gets noticed. How often have you asked a client where they work? If they wore a work shirt you wouldn't need to, so work shirts can speak on your behalf, like a silent salesperson. If you're a Plumber you will be asked more plumbing questions when you're wearing a shirt with your business name than when you're wearing your Nike shirt.

If you're opening a new business, don't wait until you are officially open for business before wearing your work shirts because you will miss countless opportunities. Every person you meet during the development or construction period is a potential client.

NEWSPAPER ADVERTISING

Newspapers are such a traditional form of external marketing, however they are also the most misunderstood. Many business owners think placing an ad is simple, however I'm here to tell you it's not. To get the most value from your advertising you need to considered the following:

- Are you advertising in the daily or weekly publication?
- Do you know the "readership"?
- Do you know the readership breakdown per day?
- Do you know the demographics of the readership?
- What section of the paper are you targeting?
- Do you want general, news or sports?

- Are you going to advertise in a feature section (such as health or business)?
- Do you want the first half of the paper or second half of the paper?
- Are you going to advertise in a lift out (such as the television guide or health guide)?
- Are you going to advertise in a promotional guide (such as a family health guide)?
- Are you doing a display ad or a line entry in the public notices?
- What size display ad will work best?
- Are you aware certain pages are more powerful than other pages?
- What position on the page have you requested?
- Do you understand what loading is?
- What is the content of your ad?
- What is the message?
- Do you know the font and layout affects how people perceive your ad?
- Who is your target market?
- Do you have one clear message or is it a mixed message?
- What is the layout of your ad?
- Did you know your business name should *not* be at the top of the ad?
- Does the ad have a strong headline?
- Is your ad in colour or black and white?

- Have you considered how your logo will look if not in colour?

- Does your logo lose recognition if it's too small?

- Are you using photographs?

- Are your photographs of high enough quality?

- How frequently will you be running your ad?

- Can you request editorial space?

- Can you create a media release to coincide with your advertising?

As you can see, newspaper advertising is more complicated than it seems, and this is why some businesses fail with newspaper advertising, because they simply get it wrong, or they listen to Sales Reps who have no idea themselves.

MAGAZINES

Advertising in magazines is similar to newspaper advertising, however they will be full colour and usually published monthly. In Cairns we have many locally published magazines, and each one is targeting a specific audience. If their target audience aligns with your target market it could be a good match. My only concern with locally produced magazines is they're usually free magazines and revenue is generated through selling advertising, so keep this in mind and *beware of sharks*. Sharks will always tell you your business is a perfect fit for their publication and readers, but who are their readers? Are they young families with kids? If so, what's one thing young families with kids don't have a lot of? Disposable income! So if your service or product relies on a target market with disposable income, this may not be the publication for you, however if your goal is to connect with young mothers then it's perfect.

Any time a magazine is free it does hold less value than a paid magazine and can therefore be picked up and read by anyone, especially C and D type clients who love freebies.

MEDIA RELEASES AND EDITORIALS

Have you ever considered why some businesses appear regularly in the newspaper and your business doesn't? The answer is simple; they submit regular media releases and editorials with high-quality content. They don't wait for media outlets to contact them; instead they actively search out stories that are newsworthy and topical.

It's important to understand the difference between a media release and an editorial, otherwise you'll fail with both. A media release should be newsworthy, and is used to provide information about a business development or event your business is involved with. Its purpose is to guide the media outlet as to how you want the story to be positioned. An editorial, on the other hand, represents your expert opinion on a particular subject that is currently relevant.

Submitting a media release or editorial used to mean you were sending it to a newspaper and magazine, however with the huge number of news-based websites, blogs and social media sites today this has changed, and you need to be aware of this. Media releases and editorials build credibility and, best of all, they are free. Journalists and Editors look for media releases and editorials that their readership will find interesting, so make sure your submissions match the readership of the outlet you are submitting to.

Journalists become annoyed if you regularly bombard them with nonsense stories that are clearly nothing more than self-promotion or simply boring, so make sure your topics are newsworthy and interesting. Use the following list as a guide for creating media releases and editorials:

- *A business milestone*: Opening, expanding or relocating an existing business, winning an award, or celebrating a business anniversary are all business milestones that should be captured with a media release.

- *Time/calendar specific*: Are there annually occurring events that your business can take a position on? Mother's Day, for example; if you own a gift store you could write an editorial about the increase or decline of certain types of gifts on this special day. If you're in the finance industry you should be commenting and taking a stance on the Federal Budget when it's handed down.

- *A charity event*: Any event that is trying to raise money or raise awareness about a specific disorder or disease is a perfect opportunity for a media release, especially if it involves children.

- *A corporate challenge*: If your business is involved in a corporate challenge, use it to your advantage and contact the media. You can light-heartedly talk your team up and explain why you'll beat the competition.

- *Introduction of a new service*: If you introduce a new service that has not previously been available in your area and it is something that will benefit the community, this is *highly* newsworthy and could be used as both a media release and an editorial.

- *Celebrity news*: Commenting on celebrities is common on social media, however if it's a big story you should jump on it as soon as possible and contact your local news outlets with your opinion, viewpoint, or solution. If a celebrity has a run in with the law and you're a Lawyer, what's your opinion?

If an incident happens on a building or renovation show and you're in the building industry, share your viewpoint and how it could have been avoided. If you're in the health industry and an athlete is injured at a major sporting event, share your thoughts on injury prevention and rehabilitation.

A media release should be no more than 250 words, and if it relates to an upcoming event it should be sent out several days beforehand so the Journalist involved has time to contact you for an interview. An editorial should be between 300 and 600 words. If you're doing an editorial, make sure you provide a good quality photograph that brings the whole editorial together; otherwise they will use a stock image that doesn't quite fit the story you're telling. With a media release you can provide photographs, but more than likely they will send out a photographer for more professional shots, plus they'll want to capture an image of the event. Always request copies of any photographs taken, as they may be useful for future marketing and can be used on social media.

Other information you need to provide in your media release:

- When did it happen or when will it happen?

- Who does it involve?

- What is the significance or why is it newsworthy?

- Who is the best person to contact for comments?

- Where is the best place for a photo opportunity?

- Supply the best contact phone numbers.

With both media releases and editorials always ask for a *tear sheet*, which is an electronic copy of the article. This is discussed further in Pillar Six.

You should find the names of all your local Journalists and add their details to your database. Send them an introductory email, letting them know who you are, your interests and where your business is located. After they reply, which they usually will, contact them via LinkedIn and add them as a business contact. Also, if you ever read an article written by a particular Journalist and you've honestly enjoyed it, send them an email telling them so. This kind gesture will be remembered.

> "Whoever controls the media, controls the mind."
>
> Jim Morrison (The Doors)

TELEPHONE DIRECTORIES

Hard-copy telephone directories are almost dead, and I should stop here and write nothing else about them, but they are still useful for lifting the height of your computer monitor on your desk. The only problem is you now need more than one directory, because it keeps getting thinner. I know some older people do still use the telephone directory, so if they're your target market then maybe it is still worthwhile, but more and more people are using their online equivalent.

Directory advertising is also not cheap, and the size of the ad will determine your costs and listing position in the directory. Our local phone book arrived last week and the only reason I still look forward to it arriving is because I'm curious to see who still places display ads, and it's always the same businesses, the ones that have not moved with the times. They'll have the biggest display ad, yet the smallest online footprint.

TELEVISION ADVERTISING

I was a huge fan of television advertising a few years ago, because living in a regional area meant advertising was relatively inexpensive and you had a captured audience, but my thinking has changed somewhat. Don't get me wrong, television still works, but it is less effective and a lot harder to get a return these days because of all the additional free-to-air channels, pay television channels and online choices now available. And you're also competing against the fast forward button on the remote control.

Of course how much you pay for an ad will vary depending on the time slot and length of the commercial. Television commercials are usually 15 or 30 seconds, and I am of the belief that if you can get your message across in 15 seconds then that's great, because it means you can place more ads (increased frequency) with the same budget.

If you're considering television advertising, especially regionally, I've always preferred early morning, daytime and late evening because it's great value for money, which means you can advertise more often. Producing a television commercial is also not as expensive as you may think – a decent television commercial can be produced for under $1000.

You may have noticed at the beginning and end of some television programs it says, *"This program has been brought to you by…"*, and it will mention a particular business. This quick message is called a *billboard* and they are free, but to receive free billboard advertising you need to run a minimum number of ads during the televised program. Billboards have fantastic impact, because many people will be in front of their televisions waiting for their program to start.

RADIO ADVERTISING

Once again, if you live in a regional area you'll find radio advertising inexpensive and quite effective because there are usually only a few commercial stations to choose from. The advantage radio advertising has over television is the low production costs and the speed at which a campaign can go to air, however there are some commonalities between television and radio advertising packages which you should be aware of.

Run-of-station ads

With both you can purchase a package called ROS (run of station), which means you buy a specific number of commercials and they will be placed randomly throughout the month. ROS packages are cost effective, however you have no control over your advertising placement.

Time-specific ads

As an alternative, both television and radio offer time-specific advertising, which means you request a specific time or program each day, and you can select the particular days of the week as well. This form of advertising is more expensive, but can be far more effective in reaching your target markets. When I first began television and radio advertising I only purchased the ROS packages, however experience has taught me that both have their merits because ROS advertising offers frequency and time-specific advertising offers reach.

Live reads and broadcasts

Radio though has a few more advertising options that television cannot match, such as live reads. A live read is when the host of the radio program reads an ad about your business during their program, usually lasting 30 to 60 seconds. If the host has a lot of credibility, it immediately gives your business credibility.

Another advertising option is a live broadcast from your business. The radio station basically sets up their radio hosts out the front of your business, and it can be combined with a sausage sizzle. I have done this myself and they are a lot of fun. It is never cheap, but it can be very effective if you've recently relocated your premises or if you have a retail arm to your business and you want to do a large promotion of new products.

Many radio stations have a prize patrol van that zips around to different business locations, usually in the mornings, promoting products, services and free giveaways. The idea of the van is to have passing motorists stop to pick up a few freebies, while at the same time promoting the location of the business they are out the front of. Whenever you're negotiating a radio campaign, make sure the Sales Rep includes the prize patrol stopping at your business as part of the deal. *If they say they cannot guarantee this will happen, don't sign the proposal.*

Talkback radio

In your area there will more than likely be a talkback radio program. If so, contact them about doing a regular segment about your business. This is quite easy to organise leading up to industry special events, however once your foot is in the door, enquire about doing a regular segment. If you can't get it for free, enquire how much it is to pay for a regular segment.

Make sure you get what you paid for

With radio and television you will receive a monthly account or statement, and on it will appear all your paid and free advertising for the month. It will show the exact time your ads ran and on what days. When you receive this, *always* compare it to your requested bookings, and if you notice an error you need to contact your Sales Rep immediately and request compensation or makeup spots. For example, you may request a group of three radio ads to be placed between 7.45 am and 8.15 am because you're targeting parents taking their children to school, but your Sales Rep couldn't get you in that specific time slot because it was already booked. Instead of contacting you and explaining the situation or asking you why you needed that particular timeslot, they move your three ads to 8.45 am to 9.15 am. To the Sales Rep you still had three ads placed, but for you it could be a lost opportunity. Never let them change your scheduled bookings without asking first, and if you let them get away with it they will do it again and again. This rule also applies if you're using a media management company or any other similar business...*keep them accountable.*

SPONSORSHIP

I remember the first sporting team I sponsored, and it was exciting seeing my business name on the back of a team shirt, but was it really sponsorship or was it a donation so they could buy team shirts? It took me many years to understand that sponsorship needs to have commercial potential, which can be leveraged to attract new clients to your business. Sponsorship should be taken seriously, and all information about the sponsorship arrangement should be in a signed agreement, detailing what you are receiving for your sponsorship dollars. Are you being offered free tickets, signage opportunities, and will your business be mentioned in media releases? Will your logo be printed on all promotional materials, and are they putting a link on their website to your website or blog?

You need to understand the group you are sponsoring so you can target your message accordingly.

Sponsorship does not have to involve a cash transaction; instead your sponsorship may involve donating time to assist with the event, or you may offer prizes or trophies. If you do offer a prize, do up a gift voucher and make sure it is *only valid for one month*. This is really important because you want an instant short-term response from the event. This is even more important if you offer this prize regularly throughout the year.

Before you agree to any form of sponsorship you need to consider the following:

- Can you get a copy of their database? Having access to their database is far more important than all the freebies they may be offering because it gives you an opportunity to make further contact, via email, mail, or both.

- What is the real cost to your business? (Gift vouchers, your time or cash.)

- What publicity will your business receive?
  - Are they advertising this event on TV?
  - Are flyers being handed out prior to the event and on the day?
  - Can you put up signage for additional exposure?

- How many people will see your business name at the event?
  - Be realistic. If you're sponsoring a local under 10's basketball team that your son or daughter plays in, consider it a donation, not sponsorship.

- Can I reach this many people with other advertising mediums? This is the most important question of all.
  - If you put the same money, time and effort into another form of marketing, would you get a better return on your investment?

Always look for opportunities; don't wait for them to come to you. In your local area there will be many sporting and social events scheduled throughout the year that attract a lot of community attention and will attract the attention of many media outlets. Offering your services at these events will cost you nothing, but will give you a lot of exposure. Contact the organisers of these events and offer your services, free of charge, then let your media contacts know that you are an event sponsor.

As the event draws closer, send media releases related to the upcoming event and how your business can benefit the participants.

If you're approached to sponsor an event and you notice the event has no major sponsor, enquire if you can have the naming rights, therefore taking ownership of the event. If it's successful, you should see if you're able to lock in a three- or five-year deal.

Alternatively, it's not hard to create your own event if you're already involved in a particular sport and you know all the right people. For example, at a grand final – whether it is for rugby, football, soccer, hockey or whatever – often there will be little to no entertainment at the half-time break, therefore enquire about having an annual "Dash for Cash", which could be a team or individual event. Because there will be hundreds of people at the grand final, your expenditure will be eclipsed by your exposure. Once again you should be able to turn this event into a newsworthy media release, especially if it can become an annual event.

> "You can't manufacture emotion. It's already there.
> When you find it – just find a way to trigger it; tap into it;
> fuel it; and watch it grow into something remarkable."
>
> Mark Harrison (Chair of the Canadian Sponsorship Forum)

As you can see, external marketing is extensive and there is a lot of crossover and linkages between various forms of external marketing and other Marketing Pillars. Sponsorship can link quite easily with a media release or editorial, and you can easily link a newspaper ad with your radio and television campaign. All external marketing can be used in your social media posts as well.

Remember, your goal with external marketing is to attract your target market to your business, and then use your internal marketing to win them over and make them raving fans of your business.

It's no secret…there's money in small business, but you must develop a cohesive relationship between your external and internal marketing.

After reading this chapter, what ideas are going through your head? Write them down *right now*.

_____

_____

_____

_____

_____

_____

_____

_____

MARKETING PILLAR FIVE: VERBAL MARKETING

I look at verbal marketing as any form of marketing that involves you opening your mouth and talking. If you get nervous meeting people for the first time or talking in front of crowds, don't be concerned – it's normal and you're not alone. I read an article once on people's fears, and public speaking was right at the top of the list, just in front of death by fire. In New Zealand it was second behind snakes…and there are no snakes in New Zealand, so figure that one out.

> "There are only two types of speakers in the world. The nervous and the liars."
>
> Mark Twain

In this chapter I will discuss the most common forms of verbal marketing and a few tips on how you can get the most out of them.

NETWORKING

I've always enjoyed networking and meeting like-minded business people who openly share their thoughts and ideas with no hidden agendas. I enjoy hearing positive news about their businesses, because as business people we're often bombarded with negative energy on a daily basis. Negative energy, day after day, can take its toll on your attitude so networking is a fantastic opportunity to get away from your business and take a dose of positive energy from people outside of your industry.

On the surface, the concept of networking is very simple. The goal is to link like-minded individuals who have a common interest together, and through relationship building and trust they become walking, talking advertisements for one another's businesses. For networking to be effective you must be genuine and honest and look at networking with a long-term view. You need to build trust with the person you're talking to. Never treat networking as a one-way promotional activity for yourself and your business. This is a networking killer. People you meet will see right through you if your only purpose in talking to them is to shove your business down their throat. Don't become *"that person"* – the one everybody in the room wants to avoid. People you meet at networking events will only refer people they know once the relationship between you is nourished and you have built trust. The best part of networking is it's one of the least expensive marketing activities you will undertake.

Some networking events are free, however others may cost you $25 to $75 depending if there's a speaker and if breakfast or lunch is included, which if you compare this to other forms of advertising is cheap. Networking is one of the most cost-effective business strategies you'll ever undertake.

It's not who you know, it's who knows you.

Not all networking events or groups are business orientated; some are community organisations such as Rotary. I was a member of Rotary for a number of years and it was a great experience. Through Rotary I met a lot of other Rotarians who became great business contacts. When you're part of a large organisation it will make it much easier for you to organise speaking engagements.

So where do you find networking groups? First you need to ask other business people, and keep your ears and eyes open and also scan the local newspaper. Most business organisations and other groups will have a regular networking meeting. For example, most towns will have a local Chamber of Commerce group or something similar.

Another type of organisation you should not overlook is the Business Women's Clubs in your area – they are amazing organisations. Yes…if you're male you can still attend, which I have done on numerous occasions with my wife Christine, and when there are 200-plus females and only a handful of males, you are going to be noticed. A good friend of mine, Scott Brown, from *Allsigns Print and Design*, is a networking genius, and each year he organises a men's table at the Business Women's Annual Christmas lunch. Are we noticed? Yes! *And after a dozen or so Christmas drinks we are noticed even more!*

Some business organisations will also have networking tables near the registrations tables, and if they do, it's always beneficial to provide some form of flyer or information brochure about your business if you have them available. It's important to remember that when you're attending a networking function you are representing your business; therefore you must always conduct yourself in a professional manner.

Opportunities for networking are only limited by your thinking, and if there's no networking group in your area, start one. Write to local business people you want to connect with and get one started. It could be before or after work, and it could be held at a favourite coffee shop. If you only have four people attend the first meeting then that's four opportunities to create long-term relationships.

Huge tip: If you're the person organising the new networking group, you initially control who is invited, therefore you don't have to invite people you do not like. Let them find out about the new networking group through other means.

> "I've learned that people will forget what you said, people will forget what you did, but people will never forget how you made them feel."
>
> Maya Angelou

DON'T HAND OUT YOUR BUSINESS CARDS

I remember the excitement I felt when I had my first business card printed. It made all the years at university seem worthwhile. I also couldn't wait to show my family and friends and start handing them out, however have you ever considered how many of your business cards go from the person's wallet to their rubbish bin within the first 48 hours? I would hazard a guess and say most of them, especially if you forced your business card on someone who didn't ask for it.

Make people want your business card

You should make people *want* your business card, but what does that really mean? Well, if you're at a networking event and someone says they have a particular problem that you know you can help resolve, before rushing in with your business card, as you normally would, stop for a moment and ask a few more questions. After they've given you more information, explain how many times you've successfully helped other people with a similar problem. Then ask how serious they are about fixing their current problem. If they say that they want it fixed immediately, tell them that you can probably help and maybe even see them in a few days if you move a few things around, then present your business card to them – but never go past half of the distance between them and you. If they want your business card they will come the other half and take the card from you.

But…here's an alternative idea if you're brave…You're at a networking event and someone says they have a problem and they ask for your business card. Once again, don't give them your card; instead ask them for more information about their problem and then take out two business cards. But, instead of giving them one, ask for their mobile telephone number. As they give you their number, write it on one business card, and on the back of the other business card write a date and a time and say, *"I'm going to call you tomorrow at 12.30 pm, during my lunch break, to make an appointment for you. Is that okay?"* If they say that would be great then they're serious about wanting their problem fixed, but if they hesitate and say, *"No it's okay, I'll call you"*, then they're wasting your time. Move on and talk to someone else!

PUBLIC SPEAKING OPPORTUNITIES

My first public speaking engagement was in front of 10 unfortunate people – and I say unfortunate because it was nothing short of abysmal. It was so bad the person who organised the talk asked me to promise to never speak in public again, and he wasn't joking. I'll admit, my confidence was low, but then I realised I could only get better, and I did. I went from abysmal to terrible, from terrible to bad, and so on.

If you have a fear of public speaking, as I did, you need to deal with it, because public speaking opens so many doors that are otherwise closed to you. Joining Toastmasters or a similar group may be able to assist you with public speaking, but for me I just threw myself in the deep end and decided I needed to sink or swim – and unfortunately I sank, but I learnt the more I did it the better I got because *everything is hard, until it's easy.* Always remember that the people you're talking to want to see you succeed, they're not there to see you fail.

Now I can talk to any size group, and I've learnt that being a little nervous before a talk or presentation is a good thing. It means you still care about the subject and your audience sees your nerves as excitement. The adrenaline hit you get after a public speaking engagement is addictive, but it's a great addiction to have and there are many long-term benefits of becoming more engaged through public speaking:

- You will come across as a *perceived expert*: remember, perception is reality.

- If you are an *expert* then the business you own and operate must also be exceptional.

- Speaking to groups of people at one time is a great way to leverage your time and promote your business for free.

- One of the best reasons why you want to say yes to a speaking opportunity: it's one less speaking opportunity for your competitors. If you don't do it, they probably will – are you okay with that?

There are a lot of organisations looking for interesting speakers, but *always keep in mind your target market. If it doesn't fit, say no.*

HAVING A BOOTH AT LOCAL SHOWS AND TRADE EXPOS

Having a booth at local shows and trade expos provides great opportunities to promote your business and the services you provide to large numbers of people in a very short period of time, however if you have a booth, make sure it looks professional, and you must make sure it is always staffed. There's nothing worse than seeing an empty booth – it does not give a good image.

Also be prepared to do a lot of talking, which is why I have placed this in verbal marketing. Most local shows and trade expos attract a lot of tyre kickers, so your primary goal is to collect names and email addresses for your database and then let your marketing systems sift through them to sort the A's and B's from the blowflies.

Some of the easiest ways to collect names and emails is by having a competition for a cool prize or offering free information, which needs to be emailed or posted.

PROMOTIONAL ITEMS

To assist in promoting your business further you must always have promotional items available that can be handed out at networking events, expos and tradeshows. Your promotional items can also be used with your internal marketing. I'm sure you will have a company in your area that produces promotional items, such as coffee mugs, pens, T-shirts, caps, golf balls and water bottles. The initial outlay can sometimes be expensive, however promotional products can be very effective when used wisely, and can make you look far bigger than you actually are. It is important to remember that these items give the receiver an impression of you and your business, so always go for quality over quantity.

DO YOU HAVE AN ELEVATOR SPEECH?

What *is* an elevator speech? An elevator speech is a concise, informative, compelling summary of who you are and what you do. Your speech needs to be told in 30 seconds or less, the same amount of time it takes for you to go from the ground floor to the tenth floor in an elevator, hence the name. It may also be used to pitch an idea, a concept, or new product.

This may sound trivial, but when you're at a networking event you will be asked *what do you do?* I'm amazed how many people are unprepared for this question. You only have a brief moment to explain yourself, and if you "um 'n' ah" the opportunity may be lost. Therefore you need to be able to communicate what you do very quickly, and you need to practise this technique. You want your elevator speech to create a spark of interest in the other person. You want them saying *tell me more.*

Extended elevator speech

This doesn't happen very often, but I've been at lunch meetings and the MC will ask if anyone would like to stand up or come on stage for one or two minutes to talk briefly about their business… it's at these times when an elevator speech, or an extended elevator speech, is needed. And what an opportunity, to get up and talk about your business in front of like-minded business people. Nothing beats free publicity, and this is why you need to always be prepared. If you practise doing this, when the opportunity arises you're going to look and sound exceptionally good and your peers will notice.

Here's a final bonus tip: ask someone to take a photo of you on stage, because this can be used on social media to build your profile and credibility. You should try to get photos at all your networking events and talks.

With all verbal marketing, it all comes back to you having the ability to talk and communicate with other people. If you don't have the skill, you need to learn it, otherwise you're gifting work and your share of the wealth pie to your competition.

Remember: *it's no secret...there's money in small business*, however you must overcome your fears.

After reading this chapter, what ideas are going through your head? Write them down *right now.*

_____

_____

_____

_____

_____

_____

_____

_____

MARKETING PILLAR SIX: ONLINE MARKETING

Online marketing is more than having a simple website about your business, though some businesses don't even have that. I tuned in to a webinar some time ago and the presenter said a staggering 53% of small businesses did not have a website. I find this surprising, however don't 50% of small business also go broke in the first two to five years? Maybe there's a correlation there.

I'll be very honest and say that up until a few years ago I thought all six Marketing Pillars were equal, however I've changed my tune a little and I now think that online marketing is the most important Marketing Pillar. You may receive a lot of professional and non-professional referrals, but I'm certain this would not be the case if you had no online marketing in place to stay in touch with them. All your Marketing Pillars are very much dependent on your online Marketing Pillar being strong. Some business owners may say that online marketing is not as important in their industry, but seriously I can't think of where this would be true.

Online marketing is cost effective and is a great way to advertise – $5000 spent on television or radio advertising can be gone within weeks, however put that same budget to work with online marketing and you could be reaping the rewards a year later. There is a plethora of online marketing ideas, which is why there are whole books written on the subject. My goal in this chapter is to give you the basics and to get you thinking about it more often. If you're already a online marketing master I congratulate you, because you've seen what many others have failed to see.

This is a fast-changing area, so it's vital that you stay up to date.

THE WEBSITE

First things first: you need to have a quality website. Previously I was talking about communication and building trust with your clients, and a website does this. It opens lines of immediate communication, and it gives the client a small insight into who you are and what you stand for. As far as I'm concerned, if a business does not have a website I do not trust the business.

When you have a website built it needs to be visually appealing, easy to navigate, and it needs regular content added because you want people coming back to your website as a reference source, and once they are there you want them to stay for as long as possible because the longer they stay on your website and the more pages they navigate through, the better Google will rank your site.

If you don't understand how rankings work, what SEO (search engine optimisation) means, and the benefits of adding regular content to your website, you need a website developer who does, and who will also educate you and will keep you informed as changes occur, not just a website developer who designs websites and then offers nothing more in updates and ongoing training. This is why having your website designed by a friend or family member is not always the best idea. Yes, it may have saved you money initially, but it could be costing you money long term without ongoing training and updates. Fortunately for me, I have two website developers I work with and use for different reasons. One is Tom Foster and the team from Foster Web Marketing in Washington DC, and the other is Nicky Jurd and the team from Precedence in Cairns. What I like most is they both keep me informed about consumer trends, changes with Google rankings, and other online changes that I need to be aware of. They are both an integral part of my business life.

> **"If you designed your own website, be careful, because even ugly kids look good to their parents."**
>
> Dr. T.

Your website should be constantly improving and evolving; it's not something you just do once and then never come back to again, though unfortunately this *is* what many business owners do. They will eagerly have a website created and maybe tweak it a few times in the first month, then forget about it. A good website developer will be in constant contact with you, reminding you to add content and when to consider updates. If you haven't changed your website for three years, make an appointment to see your website developer and discuss what changes are needed to get it up to date.

Also make sure it is responsive so it can be viewed on smartphones and tablets, because more and more people are using these devices and not traditional laptops and desktops to search for information.

When your website is firing on all cylinders you'll notice an increase in traffic and client enquiries, but never rest; constantly go back to your website and look at it as though you're a client, because techno glitches can happen.

I receive weekly emails from my website developers reminding me to add content to my blog and FAQ. I also have quarterly coaching sessions with my website developers, which is extremely helpful with working out my content strategy.

Google Analytics is also a feature you need to understand. It basically gives you detailed statistics about who is looking at your website and also web traffic to and from your website, and it also lets you know what search engines were used to find your site, how long people stayed on each particular page, whether they clicked through to another page, and if so what pages were most popular, or did they leave your site after the first click? This information is important to have because it informs you about what pages are working, which are not, and if you need to make changes. Your web developer will probably be able to help you with all this. If not, it's time to start shopping for a new developer.

COLLECTING EMAILS VIA YOUR WEBSITE

Your website should have an area where people can ask questions and request free information. You've probably seen this on other websites, where it says *click here* to receive our free report or to download our free e-book. When you do this, not only do you receive what you requested but you also receive ongoing information until you unsubscribe. If you're enjoying the information provided you'll stay subscribed, and this is their goal. They want to stay in regular contact with people until they're ready to buy. Your website needs to be set up in a similar fashion. You then need to be able to collect all the names and email addresses using a CRM (customer relationship management) program so your business can stay in regular contact with people until they're ready to become a client. Some website developers have their own CRM program that automatically collects names for you directly from your website, however if this service is not available you need to purchase a CRM program separately and enter the names and email addresses manually. There are also free CRM programs available if you search online. You should also add the names and email addresses collected at tradeshows and expos to the same CRM program.

All names and email addresses when put together become a very powerful marketing database, and that holds huge value for your business when it comes time to sell.

YOUR BLOG

You need at least one blog and this should be attached to your website, however you can have a secondary blog as well using Blogger for example, which is owned by Google, but there are many other companies offering free blog hosting. A blog is usually written by one person, however if you're part of a team your website blog may have multiple contributors and it should be updated regularly. Most blogs will centre on the services or products your business offers.

This is why you may consider a secondary blog. If you have a strong interest in something that is not related to your core business this would be an ideal blog opportunity. For example, you may be a Motor Mechanic but you have an interest in training racehorses. This secondary blog is not related to your business in any way, but it can still generate leads and contacts for your core business. Just to clarify, you wouldn't start sending information about your mechanic business to your racehorse followers, that would be wrong, but in your blog you could casually mention your mechanical background and the like, which then leads them to search you out.

Your goal with blogging is to develop followers and to create word-of-mouth marketing. You want followers telling their friends about your blog, so always be informative. The best blog articles are the ones that answer the questions going on in your clients' minds. I'll say this again because it's very important, when you write a blog it needs to *answer the questions going on in your clients' minds.* If you can answer their questions, you will have their attention. Blogs are not about your ego or opinion, and if someone leaves a comment on your blog, be responsive and reply as soon as possible.

VIDEO CONTENT

Do you need video content on your website? Yes, you do. Go online and look at the statistical data; it's mind blowing. Video is both educational and entertaining, and people will recall information they've seen on video long after viewing it, yet they will forget what they've read within days. Your website therefore needs to have video content added, ideally on each page, even if it's just a simple 30-second introductory video about the content on the page.

You can have your video content shot by a professional, and if I was shooting a television commercial this is exactly what I would do, however smartphones have HD recording capabilities and – as long as your lighting and sound are good – there's no reason why you cannot shoot your own videos for most pages on your website. Try to keep your videos short and straight to the point – a good timeframe is 30 to 60 seconds. Once you go beyond this people start to lose interest. If you're shooting an instructional video then it can go longer, or you could break it into a number of shorter videos that can be watched independently. Also, make sure you use a stable platform or tripod so you don't shoot another Blair Witch Project. There's nothing worse than shaky video, especially when it can be avoided. Don't let the editing process put you off using video. I let this hold me back for years until someone showed me how easy it was. I don't have time to go into the editing process here, so email me if you want some tips and advice *(tf@tysonfranklin.com)*.

When your video is created, make sure you get it out there for the world to see. You should upload your videos to YouTube and Vimeo. I personally prefer YouTube because Google owns You-Tube so it's always going to rank higher and be seen more often. Once your video is uploaded you can also post it to Facebook, Twitter, Pinterest and LinkedIn, which exposes your video content even further. I also like to add my videos to Blogger.

SOCIAL MEDIA

At the start of this chapter I discussed how many businesses don't have a website, which is surprising, however you do have to pay for a website so I can see why some business people put it off; they see it as an expense, not an investment. The same businesses though also don't have any social media presence, and that's *free*. Is it any wonder why they struggle? Marketing your business via social media is something you need to do because you can communicate and reach so many people in such a short period of time. I've posted articles and videos on my various business Facebook pages and within hours of posting they've reached hundreds of people, and within a few days they've reached thousands…and it costs me nothing.

Even though Facebook and Google dominate the world right now, don't discount the importance of having your business details on Yahoo, Bing and Yelp, because people search in different ways and things change quickly. I believe you should also consider having Twitter, Instagram, LinkedIn and Pinterest accounts. Once again it depends on your industry and how much time you have to dedicate towards social media. Yes, social media is free, but it does take some planning and time, and time is money.

Some people say Twitter is on the decline, but right now it's still relevant. Instagram, on the other hand, is growing in popularity, especially after it was purchased by Facebook in 2012 for one billion dollars. LinkedIn is a business-orientated social networking platform, and you should consider using it to build your own personal profile and to connect with other business people. If your business is quite visual, you should definitely consider having a Pinterest account because it attracts people with common visual interests, and it allows you to create "boards" with common themes where you can pin images or videos.

The interesting thing with social media is it's always changing. What's popular now may be gone in five years' time, but having said that, social media is here to stay, whether we like it or not. It's something you must embrace, because if you don't your younger competition will and they will use it to drive you out of business.

ONLINE DIRECTORIES

I think online directories have been popular because we grew up using the paper versions for so many years, so a lot of people still feel comfortable using them. For this reason you need to make sure your online information is correct and up to date each year.

I've personally moved away from using online directories, and I think they've lost their relevance in our modern world. However, as I write this section I did a search for Lawyers in Brisbane city on Google and this is what I was shown on page one:

- The first four listings were Google Ads.

- Then there was a map of the city, and below this was the top three law firms ranked by Google.

- Next came the Yellow Pages online directory listing.

I did the same search for Web Designers and Graphic Artists and there was no online directory listing to be found on page one, so it seems older professions, such as Law, which are ingrained with deep tradition, are also stuck in traditional old-school marketing. I would also hazard to guess that many law firms still have large ads in the printed directory, and they're confused as to why the younger, fresher firms are stealing their business.

> **"Where do you hide a dead body? Page two of Google, because nobody looks there."**

AUDIO

Even though video is hugely popular, especially short videos, I think audio is going to be just as popular in the not-too-distant future because you can easily listen to audio while you're doing another activities, whereas video requires you to stop what you're doing. Therefore, consider introducing some audio content into your online marketing.

MP3 audio recordings are easy to create, and can be easily uploaded to your website or to an online audio platform such as SoundCloud and then linked back to your website and social media pages. If you think you have a message to share there's no harm in recording your thoughts and posting them online, and sharing them with your database. And if you have a particular skill or expertise, you may be a great guest podcaster. Being a guest on someone else's podcast is a great way to lift your personal brand and business profile, plus you can use a copy of the podcast episode in your own marketing. This is why I've dived into creating my own podcast series *It's No Secret with Dr. T.*, because I know podcasting is a place I need to be; especially if I want to maintain contact with people who have read my book, such as yourself.

Can you see audio being useful in your business? It may suit some industries more than others, but I think everyone can use audio somewhere.

YOUR MOTHERSHIP

Always keep in mind that your website is like a huge mothership, where all the information about your business is stored, so regardless of where you post your written, video or audio content you always want to make reference to your website, because this is where you're trying to drive all your online traffic, back to the information source. All your advertising, both online and offline, should have details of your website, because your website holds a lot more detail about you and your business. This is where you want every potential client heading, but it also highlights why you need your website to look professional and be inviting. When clients arrive you want them to stay.

SUMMARY

This is by no means a complete list of everything that needs attention when it comes to online marketing, but it's a good starting point. This book is all about making money in small business, and even though online marketing is one of the last chapters of the book this should really be one of the first things you get organised.

When I truly understood online marketing my business flourished. Some online marketing is very simple, and in all honesty it only takes a few hours each week to get it organised. If you cannot afford a few hours then outsource this task to someone else, but either way it needs to get done.

To get the best results from all your marketing you need to work on all six Marketing Pillars, not just one or two, or the ones you feel comfortable with – you need to work on all of them simultaneously to get the best results. Individually each pillar is good; but together they are awesome.

Remember: *it's no secret…there's money in small business,* however you need to have a huge online footprint.

After reading this chapter, what ideas are going through your head? Write them down *right now.*

_____

_____

_____

_____

_____

_____

_____

_____

CREATE YEARLY
MARKETING FOLDERS

In 1994 I started keeping copies of all my advertising and marketing – and I mean *everything*. Not just ads placed in the newspaper, but copies of editorials, brochures, newsletters and even a copy of my business card at that time. As this information grew, I decided I had to keep it in some sort of orderly fashion and so began the process of creating *marketing folders* each year. I still look through these folders on a regular basis for inspiration.

You should start your marketing folder as soon as possible and keep it up to date. Marketing items should be added in chronological order, and it's best to divide the folder into monthly sections. When you add an item, attach handwritten notes, especially if there was something unique you want to remember in the future. If your folder is full before the end of the year, it means you're keeping busy.

I know, I know...you could use your computer to scan and save all your marketing activities instead of using a folder, and I did do this for a short period of time myself, but it doesn't have the same impact as seeing your marketing folders grow, year by year, along your bookshelf. Hard-copy folders are also easier to review. If business ever slows, immediately turn to your marketing folder. Is it full or is it looking a little thin?

Here is a list of what needs to be included in your marketing folder:

- Television and radio schedules: *Your Sales Rep will provide you with these schedules.*

- Newspaper ads and editorials: *Record the page number, the date and the day of publication. Also note down if the weather was poor. Bad weather does affect outcomes.*

- Media releases: *As above with newspapers.*

- Online directories: *Once again, add a copy to the month it became live, and add additional copies if it is changed in any way during the contract period.*

- Copies of blogs, FAQs and so on: *As above with online directories.*

- Copies of all printed materials: *If you do a letterbox drop or distribute brochures and flyers, record details regarding distribution areas and quantity.*

- Sponsorship information: *If you sponsor a team or individual, add a copy of your agreement, and when it comes to a conclusion, record your thoughts regarding the positives and negatives of this sponsorship arrangement and if you would do it again.*

- Networking and business functions: *After every networking event, you should note who you met and what you learnt from the evening. Also, was it a worthwhile function and would you attend again?*

- Community talks and presentations: *Note what went well and what you would change. Record the organiser's contact details for future reference.*

- Client letters: *Every formatted letter you use for contacting clients or reactivating clients should be added in the month it was created. Every time you make a change, no matter how small, a new copy should be added. If you're making a lot of changes you may want to use a separate folder to store all your outgoing letters so they don't get lost among other marketing activities.*

- Professional and non-professional referrer personal visits: *Every meeting should be recorded and also your feelings about the meeting.*

- Email or SMS marketing: *If you do a group email or SMS to your clients, professional referrers or anyone else, make sure you keep a copy. I like to keep copies of my emails and SMSs in the same folder as my letters.*

- Information evenings: *You should note down the topic for the evening, a list of everyone invited, how many RSVPs were received, and who did not attend.*

If you're unsure if an item should go into your marketing folder then it probably should because it can always be removed at a later date.

Regardless of how well you track your marketing, the quote below by John Wanamaker (1838–1922) is important to remember.

"Half my advertising is wasted, I just don't know which half."

John Wanamaker

This quote has stood the test of time and is still talked about today, because when John Wanamaker died he had a net worth of over a billion dollars in today's money, and he did this knowing that only half his advertising worked. With today's technology we have the ability to be far more accurate in determining the effectiveness of our marketing, however you need to be diligent and you need to care.

MONTHLY REFERRAL SOURCES

Every new client should be asked how he or she heard about your business, and this information needs to be as accurate as possible. Regardless of what a client writes on their information sheet, you need to enquire a little further because you want accurate information. If they write word of mouth, this is too vague; you need to ask more questions.

You should print your "referral sources" each month and add this information to your yearly marketing folder. You should see patterns developing between your monthly referrals and your ongoing marketing activities. You will be surprised where your referrals come from, which is why it's important to record all your marketing activities, not just the ones you think are important.

MARKETING DIARY FOR NEXT YEAR

At the end of each year I like to set a few days aside and reflect on the previous year's marketing activities. I find this process quite enjoyable, and it can be a rewarding exercise to do with other team members, especially if they have been involved in the thought process. If time permits, go back and look at the past five years, and after reviewing these folders, use this information to develop your marketing plan for the next 12 months.

As each year passes you'll notice successful marketing ideas will be repeated, which makes planning for the upcoming year much easier. It's also important to evaluate your marketing ideas that did not go well and try to learn from them so you do not repeat the same mistake.

I think it's important to also highlight public holidays and other significant days throughout the year in your marketing diary, such as Mother's Day and Father's Day, St Patrick's Day and the football finals, just to name a few, and plan some of your marketing around these days. In my business I had 12 different email signatures designed to use at different times throughout the year. I did this for a bit of fun, but they were noticed and often commented on. I also used these email signature themes on social media.

Using a marketing diary for the year is one of the best ways to keep you and your team focused and on track for what needs to be done each week and month, but remember your plans are set in sand, not concrete – you do have the ability to make changes as the weeks and months progress based on results.

It's no secret…there's money in small business, but you must reflect on the past, learn from the present and plan for the future.

After reading this chapter, what ideas are going through your head? Write them down *right now*.

_____

_____

_____

_____

_____

_____

_____

CONCLUSION

Take a close look at your profession or industry and you'll realise that there are some people making some ridiculous amounts of money, which is why *it's no secret...there's money in small business.* However, for you to achieve this, you must first believe it is truly possible. Without belief you have nothing.

I attended a business seminar in 1998 with about 100 other people, and the speaker asked everyone to write down how much money they would like to earn in the next financial year. He then asked everyone to write down all the things they needed to change in their personal and work life to make this income goal a reality. He explained how we only needed to make minor changes in our thinking and in our actions to make this goal a reality, which made perfect sense.

Then, just as I was getting comfortable with my new income goal, he said, "Okay, now I want you to triple it." The room exploded, and my initial thought was, *"You're kidding me aren't you?"* But as he continued to talk I understood the point he was trying to make. To achieve a small goal, a goal just out of your reach, you only need to make small changes, but to achieve a much bigger goal, such as tripling your income in 12 months, you would have to make much bigger changes, and in some cases massive changes.

You need to understand how your mind works. Small goals will not push you mentally, because you already know they can be achieved with little or no additional effort, however larger goals require you to think and act vastly differently. To achieve a goal like tripling your income, you must first believe you can do it, and once you believe it is a possibility only then will you take all the necessary steps required for its attainment.

Thank you for reading my book. I do hope you've enjoyed the journey as you moved through each chapter. I would love any feedback you may have and would also love to hear some of your success stories along the way, so when you can, please email me at tf@tysonfranklin.com.

**"Never get so busy making a living
that you forget to make a life."**

NOW WHAT?

WEEKLY NEWSLETTER

Right now could be the moment where you change your life forever, or it could be a moment that simply passes you by and is forgotten: the decision is yours. If you're feeling motivated you need to take action immediately. Don't wait until tomorrow, or next week, instead head straight to Tyson Franklin's website and register for his FREE newsletter: www.tysonfranklin.com.

Tyson's newsletter will give you tips and ideas you can use immediately in your business that will generate instant profits. If you are not yet in business for yourself but you're thinking about it, register anyway; you won't be disappointed.

ARE YOU LOOKING FOR A SPEAKER AT YOUR NEXT EVENT?

If you're looking for a speaker to educate and motivate your team or organisation, Tyson Franklin will tick all the boxes. On his website you'll find a list of topics he regularly talks about, but be warned, Tyson is not a boring speaker; he will keep your attendees entertained, and before they realise they'll walk away fully charged and motivated to achieve more than they ever thought possible. Tyson has been presenting for well over 20 years, and has had the privilege of speaking throughout Australia, New Zealand, Fiji and North America. He loves nothing more than sharing his knowledge with others. For more details visit his website www.tysonfranklin.com and download his speakers kit.

ONE-ON-ONE COACHING

Tyson is also available to coach a limited number of one-on-one clients, however this option is only available if you are serious about wanting to build an awesome business that stands out from the crowd. Send Tyson a direct email if you want to know more about one-on-one coaching: tf@tysonfranklin.com

> "Change is hard at first, messy in the
> middle and gorgeous at the end."
>
> Robin Sharma

THE PODCAST SERIES

If you want to earn more, work less and enjoy what you do each day, then you need to subscribe and tune into this weekly podcast series, where Tyson E. Franklin (a.k.a. Dr. T.) has guests from all over the world, sharing their thoughts and experiences in all aspects of life and business.

The goal of this podcast is to have open and honest conversations and for you to be able to take away information that will make your personal and business life better.

Printed by BoD™in Norderstedt, Germany

9 781925 648416